OVEN TEMPERATURES

GAS	½	1	2	3	4	5	6	7	8	9
FAHRENHEIT	275°	300°	325°	350°	375°	4				
CENTIGRADE	135°	149°	163°	177°	190°	2				

WEIGHTS

BRITISH	½ oz	1 oz	2 oz	3 oz	4 oz	8 oz / ½ lb	16 oz / 1 lb	32 oz / 2 lb
METRIC (approx)	15g	30g	60g	90g	120g	240g	480g	Not quite 1 kilo
AMERICAN		¼ stick	½ stick		1 stick	2 sticks	4 sticks	8 sticks

MEASURES

Imperial Pints & Fluid ounces	1 fl oz	2 fl oz	3 fl oz	4 fl oz	5 fl oz	6 fl oz	7 fl oz	8 fl oz	9 fl oz	½ pt / 10 fl oz
Metric (approx)	30 ml	60 ml	90 ml	120 ml	145 ml	170 ml	200 ml	230 ml	260 ml	280 ml
AMERICAN		¼ cup		½ cup				1 cup		

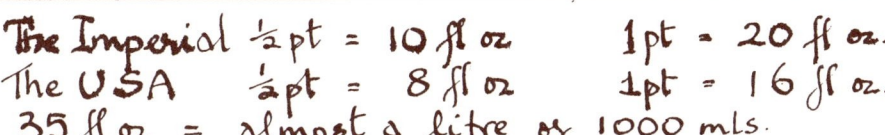

```
The Imperial   ½ pt = 10 fl oz      1 pt = 20 fl oz
The USA        ½ pt = 8 fl oz       1 pt = 16 fl oz
35 fl oz = almost a litre or 1000 mls.
```

The American measuring tablespoon is smaller than the British, so use an American tablespoon plus a teaspoon = 1 Br. tablespoon. American measuring teaspoons are also smaller than British.
4 British tablespoons = 2½ fl oz.
13 British tablespoons = 8 fl oz (ie ½ a U.S. pint)

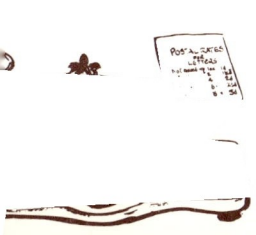

BANQUETING

for

ONE

(If you are more ~ multiply!)

hand written and illustrated by the author

JOAN WOLFENDEN

Of this first edition of 4,000 books, 1,000 have been numbered & signed by the author
NO: 956

Joan Wolfenden

By the same author   RECIPES to RELISH.
The GLORY of the GARDEN
The SATISFACTION of STITCHERY
with Madeleine Masson: The GRAND SALAD

First published in Great Britain by Peacock Vane, Bonchurch, Isle of Wight.
Copyright © Joan Wolfenden 1985

All rights reserved. No part of this publication may be reproduced, stored in a retrieval system or transmitted in any form or by any means, electronic, mechanical, photo copying, recording or otherwise, without the prior permission of the copyright owner.

ISBN 0 9506749 4 X

Produced by CROSSPRINT NEWPORT, ISLE of WIGHT

TABLE of CONTENTS

SOUPS

Almond	75
Avgolemono	73
Avocado	45
Carrot and Orange	76
Celery, Apple & Tomato	74
Chicken and Parsley	36
Chicken stock	9
Cucumber	77
Croutons	10
Mushroom	29
Mutton broth	28
Onion	76
Parsnip	22
Pea	67
Pumpkin	30
Quick Nourishing	16
Skate	44
Summer	59
Sweetcorn	25
Tomato	44
Vegetable broth	10
Vegetable consommé	56, 66
Watercress	76

SALADS

Aubergine	19
Avocado	13
Avocado Mbaroki	45
Beetroot and Onion	12
Cauliflower	65
Chicken	8
Chicory and Orange	15
Cole slaw	12
Cucumber, courgette & melon	37
Cucumber and dill	24
Green	8
Marrow	68
Melon	14
Potato Mayonnaise	8
Runner or French bean	63
Russian	66
Tomato	40

EGG DISHES

Belgian Omelettes	80, 81
Curried Eggs	84
Madeira Egg	78
Piperade	80
Poached Eggs Florentine	19
Russian Eggs	86
Spanish Omelette	21
Tagliatelle verdi	40
Torta pasqualina	73

SAUCES

Béchamel	33
Cheese	77
Cucumber	24
Cream vinaigrette	13
Curry	81
French dressing	8
Garlicky Tomato	42
Mayonnaise	9
Tarragon or mint cream	13
Tartare	15

CHEESE DISHES

Buck rabbit	78
Cauliflower cheese	66
Cheese and Semolina Soufflé	54
Cheese spread	77
Risotto	84

SHORT CUTS 96

Beurre manié	20, 60
Clover	59, 60
Colander	62
Duxelle	29, 52
How to chop an onion	82
Keeping vegetables in the fridge	24
Oil pot and brush	55
Poppadums	84
Seasoned flour	54
Vanilla sugar	89

PUDDINGS

Almond paste	87
Atholl brose	90
Chocolate Sauce	91
Cocoanut ice	88
Cocoanut shortbread	89
Crème chantilly	89
Fudge	88
Melon Fruit Salad	14
Orange cheese cake	90
Petits fours	87
Pumpkin ramekin	30
Rum soufflé	10
Syllabub	90

POULTRY

Chicken	boiled	7
	cold	14
	curry	84
	devilled legs	39
	pancakes	20
	Malaysian spiced	22
	with sweetcorn	23
	thighs	70
Petti di Pollo alla Valdestramo		60
Poussin		61
Quail		38

VEGETABLES

Asparagus	58
Aubergine	18
Baked jacket potatoes	12
Beetroot	23
Brown rice	42
Brussels sprouts	63
Cabbage with mace	64
Cauliflower	65, 66
Celery	68
Chicory, fried	15, 36
French beans	62
French beans and bacon	63
Leeks	17
Lettuce, braised	21
Marrow	68
Mixed roots	55
Potatoes (almost chips)	64
" and Jerusalem artichokes	34
" Lyonnaise	65
" mashed	65
" Sauté or fried	65
Parsnip	22
Purple sprouting broccoli	67
Red cabbage	50
Runner beans	63
Risotto	84
Spinach	69
Sugar peas	67
Swedes and turnips	69
Sweetcorn	25
Vegetable bake	45

MENUS

For entertaining a special guest	93–95

FISH

Cod Steak Portugaise	34
Crab à l'Americaine	46
Crab rumble tumble	47
Curried fish	83
Dressed crab	47
Fillet of plaice or haddock	15
Fish pie	33
Lobster loaf	56
Lobster oregano	79
Moules marinière	31
Mussel cocktail	32
Pasta with smoked haddock	16
Prawns, empanadina	37
" curried	83
Salmon steak, poached	58
Scallops Billingsgate	48
" with fresh haddock	49
Scampi thermidor	32
Skate, black butter	43
Smoked herring	86
Sole en goujeons	78
Trout with fennel	35

MEAT

Beefburgers	72
Boeuf Wellington	52
Chicory & Ham au gratin	15
Claret balls	72
Escalope of Veal or Pork	57
Gammon steak	53
Ham with leek	17
Jambon sauce Madeire	44
Kidneys	36
Lamb chop à l'Italienne	42
" cold	27
" curried	83
" onion or cucumber	27
" with peppers	53
" roasted	26
Liver with onions	71
Mince with a difference	39
Moussaka	18
Marrow stuffed with sausage	68
Pork chop with apple & cider	49
" grilled	18
Risotto	85
Tournedos flambé	51
Steak, fillet maître d'hôtel	28

What a lot of us live alone – bachelors – both men and women, one parent families, and most of all we widows.   Cooking for one can be a bore. But, variety truly is the spice of life and simplicity the most successful rule.   Both extravagant and economic dishes can be made easily and quickly. Also dishes that cost little are sometimes the more delicious ~~~ Eating at home will nearly always be pounds in hand on eating out!   We don't have the same overheads as caterers and with a little "know how" magic meals can be produced in a scant 20 minutes ~ that's the time it takes to boil a potato and during that time a chop can be grilled and a green vegetable or a salad prepared.   It takes about twenty minutes to enjoy one good dish and the two periods should balance. But, like all rules, they are made to be broken and there are always exceptions.

So, here follows a mixture of dishes. Jumble them together as fancy and the purse dictates and enjoy living alone. That's my philosophy and I hope you will find my repertoire interesting.   When you entertain your friends just multiply the ingredients.

Yaffles. Spring 1984

Often I am asked to talk to womens clubs. Sometimes a few brave men are present! Here are five meals from one small boiled chicken. There is no need to eat them all the same week. The ingredients for the other four variations on the theme can be stored in polythene bags in the freezer compartment of the fridge for later use. Do label them, though. I always know I will remember and then am mothered by a stone object of dubious origin! ~~~

Boiled Chicken. If you use a frozen one, thaw for at least 2 days in the fridge. This is important, both for the flavour & for health reasons. Cook in a well covered pot on the top of the cooker in barely simmering water. I use about 1 pint. After ½ an hour add a teaspoon of sea salt, a chopped potato or a tablespoon of rice, half an onion, chopped, a little cut up celery, a diced carrot and any other rootcrops. Simmer for a further half hour. Take out the chicken and carve off a nice portion and put it on to a hot plate. With a slotted spoon take out the vegetables and place with the chicken. In a small pan melt ½ oz butter and stir in a level dessertspoonful of plain flour. Add a little of the chicken water and a little milk. Stir in a tablespoonful of chopped parsley ~ stems too ~ bring to the boil and pour over the chicken and the vegetables.

Chicken Salad.
   Cut off a leg and a thigh and make a really good potato mayonnaise. If you are one of the "wise virgins" you will have boiled too many potatoes the day before and then you won't have to cook some specially. Chop some fresh mint and cut chives fine with scissors. Mix with mayonnaise, or salad cream. A dash of real cream adds a touch of magic. Stir together well.

Green Salad.   You don't really need a recipe, do you?
   I like to use: the heart of a lettuce, water cress, chicory, grated raw carrot, cucumber, tomato, chives and parsley, chopped. A little crunchy chopped celery & some slices of sweet pepper. Do not dress until the last moment else it will flop!

For the dressing I use:
Olive oil - about 4 oz, salt, a teaspoon of made mustard, a teaspoon of sugar, plenty of freshly ground black pepper, a tablespoonful of wine vinegar or lemon juice. Stir well and keep in the fridge. I like to add an egg into this brew. Shake well!

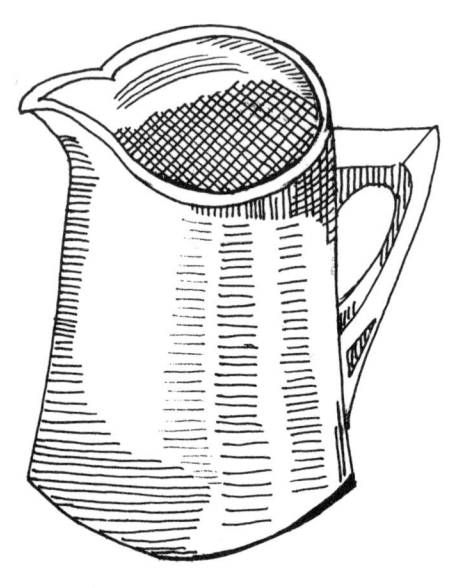

Mayonnaise can be made very quickly using a hand electric whisk. Mix in a dry basin 1 egg yolk, a saltspoon of salt, pepper, teaspoon dry mustard. Mix thoroughly by hand. Now, using the whisk gradually add 4 oz olive oil and a tablespoonful of wine vinegar or lemon juice.

Don't forget that real champagne can be bought in ¼ bottles!

Of course, not everyday. But if you want to feel festive then a certain amount of props make all the difference ~ ~ ~

Take the rest of the chicken off the bone and make it into three polythene parcels for the freezer part of the fridge. Put the bones back in the stock and Simmer. This needs to be boiled up everyday adding more water if necessary. It should set into a beautiful jelly.

Vegetable Broth.

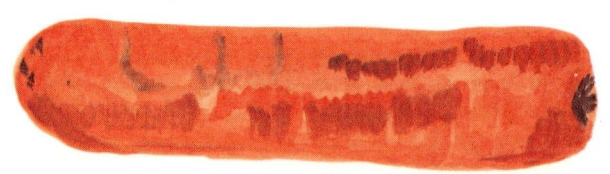

Any root crops. (Potato, carrot, leek, turnip, swede, celery, artichoke, parsnip, onion et cetera).
Some dried vegetables: porridge oats, lentils et cetera.
Chop the onion, cut the root crops small, add some oats or lentils. Cover with ¾ pint stock and simmer for 20 minutes. Add salt & pepper to taste, sprinkle with grated cheese and enjoy it.

This is sufficient for two good servings. It is good the second time served with croutons instead of cheese. Cut a stale slice of bread, crusts and all, into little squares and toss in a buttered pan until golden and crisp. Bacon fat or sausage fat makes excellent croutons. Toss into the hot plate of soup and they should sizzle.

Such a meal calls for an interesting pudding. Rum soufflé Omelette.

If you have no rum, sweet sherry or vermouth can be used.

Separate the white of an egg from the yolk.

In a tiny pan make the sauce. Use a dessert spoon as a measure. 1 spoon butter. Cut off a little for the frying pan and melt — this is to cook the omelette in. Now a spoonful of rum (or similar) and a spoonful of demerara sugar. Seethe and take off heat. Whip the white stiff, whip in the yolk, tip into the buttered frying pan and cook just long enough to form a skin underneath. Fold up and slide on to a warm plate. Reheat the sauce and pour it over. The whole cooking and preparing time should take less than five minutes if you are organised.

January: FEASTING. Occupation of the months. from the Calendar of the Playfair Book of Hours. French; late 15th century. (Kind permission of the Victoria & Albert Museum).

11

In Winter lettuce is apt to be expensive. Two reasonable salads for this season ~ which will keep well in the fridge for a second or even third appearance are:

Beetroot & Onion Salad.
　　Alternate layers of sliced cooked beetroot and very thinly sliced rings of raw onion. Arrange in a screw topped jar ~ preferably with a plastic lid and pour over a little wine vinegar and water boiled with a dessertspoonful of red currant jelly. Delicious served with cold meat and baked jacket potatoes:

You can see how fast the butter melted ~

Cole Slaw. There are many different recipes for this salad. My favourite one is: Use half white and half red cabbage. Shred finely and mix.

12

Soak for at least an hour in French dressing. The bulk should reduce by half as the dressing attacks and breaks down the cabbage. Add chopped chives, or a little finely chopped raw onion, chopped apple and/or celery, slices of raw mushroom, and a few chopped nuts. It is possible to buy small quantities of flaked almonds. Again keeps well in the fridge.

Avocado pear makes a simple and festive starter. Here is one of Rosalind's recipes.

First make the dressing. (This, too, will keep in the fridge in a jar) 1 egg. 2 tablespoons caster sugar, 3 tablespoons white wine vinegar. 1 tablespoon chopped herbs (tarragon or mint). Salt, pepper and 2 tablespoons whipped cream.

Except for the cream, whisk all the ingredients together over a low heat in a very thick small saucepan. As the mixture thickens draw it away from the heat and leave to cool. Fold in the cream. Either pour into & over the avocado ~ or peel the fruit and chop and mix into the dressing. This dressing made with mint is equally good as a starter with melon. It can either be poured over a section or the melon can be cut into balls with a gadget.

If you have melon to spare, cut into cubes or balls, it is a beautiful basic ingredient of fresh fruit salad. Add a banana cut in rings and any other fruit, strawberries, raspberries, apple, pear, — the choice is endless and only limited by the seasons. Anointed with a squeeze of lemon juice and sprinkled with sugar it is ready very quickly.

To make the cold chicken different eat it with a slice of ham. A particulary good winter salad is made of chicory and orange.
Cut the chicory into rings & the peeled orange into slices. This is best dressed with French dressing made with orange juice instead of lemon — although

the ordinary dressing is quite all right if you have it mixed ready.

Another good winter dish is to roll a chicory in a slice of ham and place it in a buttered small oven dish and cover with cheese sauce. Bake in a medium oven until bubbling and golden brown — it takes about 25 minutes.

Chicory is delicious cut into four lengthways. Fry it briefly. It is a quick supper dish with eggs and bacon.

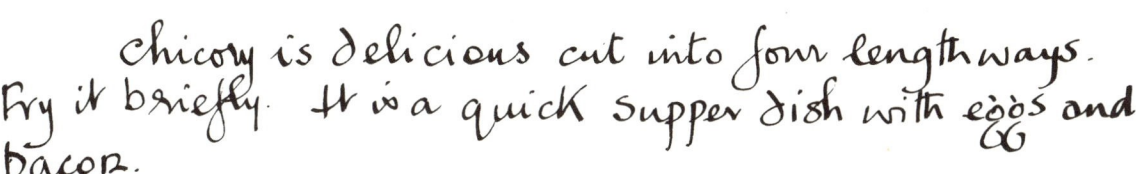

A fillet of plaice or fresh haddock dipped in beaten egg and dried with breadcrumbs will fry in a shallow pan with potatoes (already boiled) cut into suitable shapes & is greatly enhanced with home made tartare sauce. Cut up chives or onion, gherkins, capers and some tomato and mix into mayonnaise. This too, will keep in a jar in the fridge.

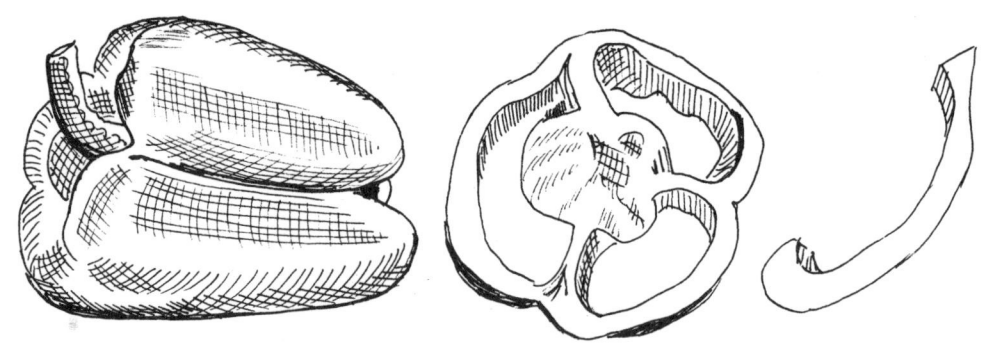

Pasta with Smoked Haddock and Peppers

Cut some green pepper into strips and cook with a handful of pasta (any shape is suitable) until done but not soft and squidgy. Poach a piece of smoked haddock in milk. Keep the milk. Make into a sauce with butter, flour and grated cheese. Flake the haddock and stir into the sauce. Put the pasta and peppers into a buttered dish, pour over the haddock mixture. Sprinkle with more grated cheese and flash under the grill until golden brown and bubbling.

This dish goes well with crisp wholemeal toast.

A Quick Nourishing Soup.

Cut an onion or a leek small and start it off in a small saucepan (with a good fitting lid) with a little butter or vegetable oil. Add a rasher of streaky bacon cut small and fry briefly. Add a small tin of baked beans and a little stock or vegetable water. Cover and simmer for about five minutes and having poured it into a soup plate sprinkle with chopped parsley and grated cheese.

Leeks may be used instead of chicory in the ham and cheese dish. Some palates prefer the leeks blanched in boiling water for about 5 minutes before wrapping them in the ham.

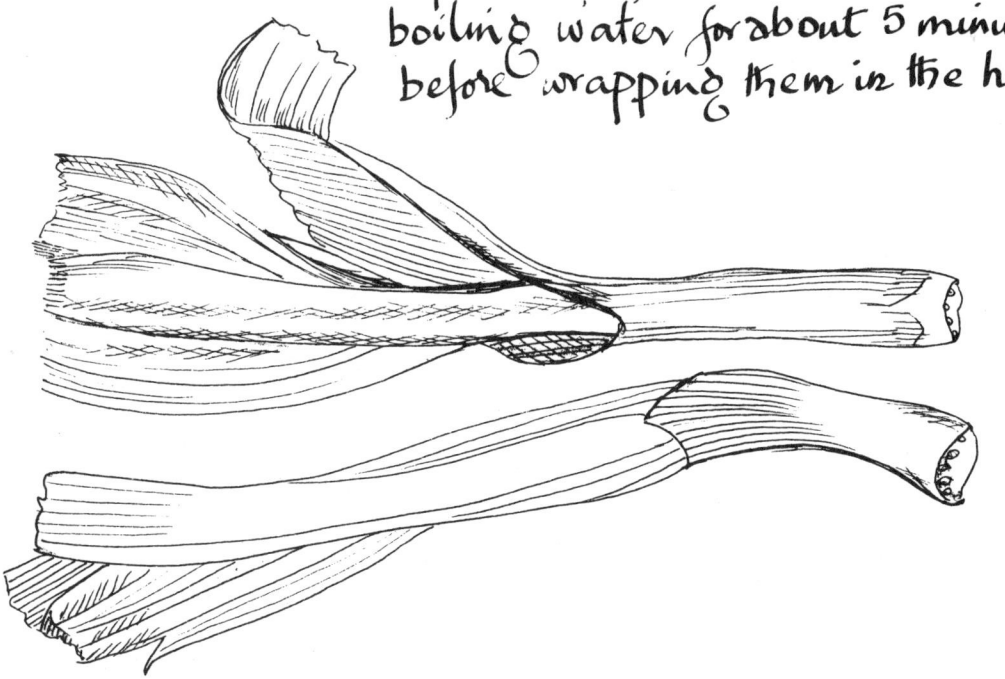

Leeks are good cooked without water. Use 4 onion chopped, a leek washed and cut into rings, a carrot cut in very thin rings and a dessertspoonful of butter.
Start the onion off first in the butter. Low heat lid on. After about 5 minutes add the rest of the ingredients, simmer very gently until tender. This vegetable goes very well with a grilled pork chop.

Grilled Pork Chop.   Mince a fresh slice of bread, sprinkle with a little sage, salt and pepper.   Cut ¼ onion fine and boil briefly — Keep the water and add the onion and half an apple, cut small, to the bread.   Grease a baking tin.   Mould the bread under the chop and Grill.   Turn the chop so as to cook the other side & leave the bread to crisp up under the heat.

Aubergine may be used in many different ways.   They are the principal ingredient of MOUSSAKA.   This dish is often very badly cooked but can be delicious.   It is NOT a Greek shepherd's Pie!
    Cut 4 slices of aubergine (unpeeled & about ¼" thick).   Brush with oil. Fry briefly, brush the other side and fry this too.   Place two slices in the bottom of a very small buttered oven dish. In the oily pan fry a little onion and after a few minutes add a chopped tomato. Season with salt, pepper and a pinch of marjoram — or thyme.   Add some cooked chopped lamb (not minced) or some raw lamb cut small. Stir together and place on top of the aubergine.   Cover

with the other two slices aubergine and a generous amount of cheese sauce. (p.77) Bake in a moderate oven for at least 20 minutes. It is best after 35-40 minutes.

AUBERGINE SALAD (A Turkish recipe)*

Cover the rest of the aubergine in foil and grill, turning after 10 minutes. Put under the cold tap, take off the foil and peel off the skin. Liquidise and add the juice of ½ a lemon. Now add oil very slowly stirring until a lot is absorbed. This can be flavoured with garlic. Eat as a spread with hot buttered toast. Salt, pepper and chives may be added to please your palate.

*I am told the Turkish name for this salad means: "The Priest Wept." This was her extravagant use of oil!

POACHED EGGS Florentine.

Cook ¼ lb spinach in the water that clings to it after washing. It takes about 4 minutes. Strain and cut with a sharp knife in the colander. Butter a fireproof dish, put in the spinach, put two poached eggs on top and some cheese

sauce (p.77.) Flash under the grill to give the cheese sauce a golden brown, bubbling appearance.

Let us return to the chicken in the freezer part of the fridge.   Chicken Pancakes.   I ate these first on the coast in East Africa.

Make a pancake in the usual way. Pancake mixture keeps for several days in the fridge in a screw topped jar.   For the filling take some of the less attractive cuts of the chicken and cut small - scissors are best! Make a white sauce, half chicken stock, half milk and a spoonful of beurre manié.

Beurre manié is the cook's best friend. It is equal quantities of plain flour and soft butter stirred together. It can then be kept in the fridge and is instantly ready. It will thicken anything and never goes lumpy.

Add a dessertspoonful to the stock and milk and boil until it is smooth and the flour cooked. It should be stirred constantly   Fry some onion and tomato with parsley and thyme, add the chicken and a little of the sauce. Stuff the pancake and roll it up Cover with more sauce, and if liked a little grated cheese. Grill until very hot.   Eat with a salad or a suitable vegetable.

The outside leaves of a lettuce are good shredded and cooked with a little chopped onion in a teaspoon of butter. Simmer closely lidded for about 10 minutes and then drop in a knob of beurre manié, salt and pepper. This absorbs the natural juices and tastes very good.

Spanish Omelette.   Beat three eggs together. In a very small fryingpan cook slices of onion and very thin slices of raw potato in a dessertspoonful of oil.   Now add whatever you fancy. Usually I use shreds of green or red sweet peppers, streaky bacon (or ham) cut very small, a tomato, chopped, cooked peas or french beans.   Just about anything goes. Pour in half the eggs and set on the bottom.   Pour on the rest of the eggs and flash under the grill to set the top.   Now enjoy half the omelette served hot. The other half is delicious eaten cold with a tasty salad.

Parsnips can add variety to meals. I like them cut into fingers, just lightly boiled, fried in sausage fat served with old fashioned mashed potatoes and some of the sausages which supplied the fat!

Curried Parsnip Soup.
Peel and dice half a parsnip in a dessertspoonful of butter with a little chopped onion and a rub of garlic until softened but not brown. Add a level dessertspoonful of plain flour and a pinch of curry powder and gradually add ½ pint of hot stock (beef is best but the chicken will do). Simmer until the vegetables are cooked. Then liquidise or pass through a mouli-légumes. Taste and add sea salt and black pepper to your liking. Add a little cream and chopped chives. This soup is a meal in itself.

Malayan Spiced Chicken. This is very MILD.
This should not be "hot" but pleasantly spiced. You need some really strong chicken stock and a handful of chopped, cooked chicken. Fry together ½ oz butter

and a teaspoonful of curry powder. Add a dessertspoonful of dessicated cocoanut, a slice of onion finely chopped, a handful of sultanas or currants, a tablespoonful of fruit syrup (of ½ quantity of jam or jelly) and ¼ pint of stock. Add a small cooking apple thinly sliced and simmer all together until thickish. Add the chicken and heat thoroughly. Serve with rice, chutney and rings of fresh banana.

For the chicken's Final Curtain:
Make a sauce of ½ chopped onion cooked in chicken stock and a tablespoon of beurre manié, salt and pepper. Use a small tin of sweet corn. In a buttered oven dish put a layer of chopped chicken, cover with sauce and top with a layer of corn. Repeat again & finally cover with mashed potato or a pastry crust. Bake until golden brown and bubbling. (About 20 mins) (Pastry 35 mins)

Beetroot.
Served hot makes a good Winter vegetable. They will cook exactly the same as a baked jacket potato

and are delicious with a knob of butter and something very simple such as liver and bacon and mashed potatoes. They peel very easily once cooked and take about an hour in a medium hot oven.

Cucumber

If you buy ½ a cucumber you can make sandwiches for tea, a cucumber salad using French dressing and sprinkling with dill seed, and a cucumber sauce to garnish a lamb chop.

Sauce: 1 heaped teaspoon soft butter & a similar quantity of plain flour. Cook a little onion in a little butter or oil and then add the other butter and flour & stir together. Add 2 tablespoons of milk and a few slices of cucumber cut small. Peel left on is best. Simmer for about 10 minutes and taste for salt and pepper needed.

This sauce is very good with a grilled Scotch salmon steak, new potatoes and peas.

Small pieces of cucumber, root crops etc., can be kept in first class condition for several days, housed in an ice cream container at the bottom of the fridge. Mixed together, pieces can be taken out as they are needed. Add kitchen paper and change often. Always keep the lid on.

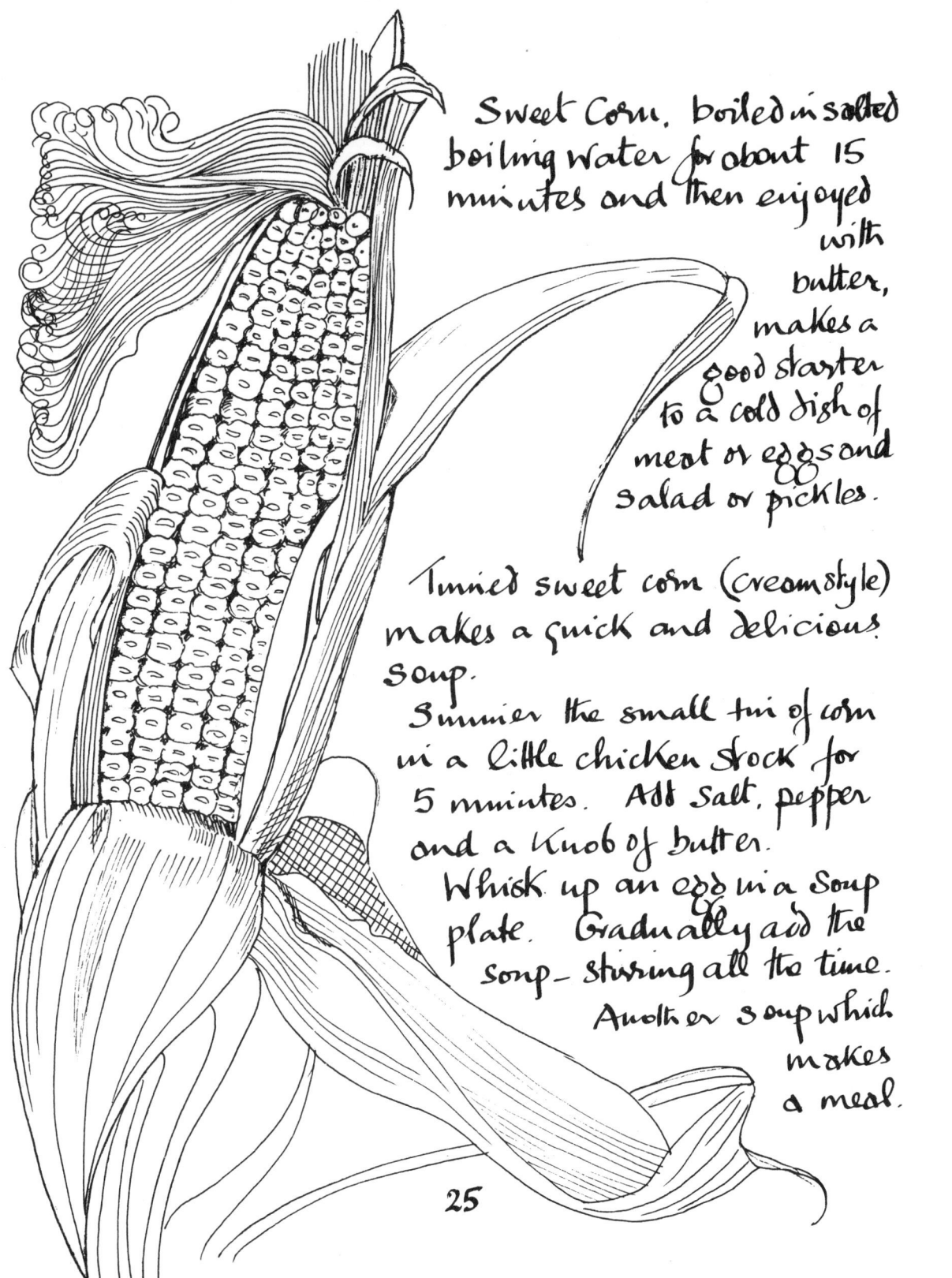

Sweet Corn, boiled in salted boiling water for about 15 minutes and then enjoyed with butter, makes a good starter to a cold dish of meat or eggs and salad or pickles.

Tinned sweet corn (cream style) makes a quick and delicious soup.

Simmer the small tin of corn in a little chicken stock for 5 minutes. Add salt, pepper and a knob of butter.

Whisk up an egg in a soup plate. Gradually add the soup — stirring all the time.

Another soup which makes a meal.

A shoulder of Lamb is as versatile as the boiled chicken.

    First enjoy a roast. This is the time to ask a friend in: Cut a small onion, a turnip and a carrot quite small. Grease an oven tin. Cook the mixed vegetables for about 5 minutes. Strain and keep the water. Mound the vegetables in the middle of the tin and place the shoulder on top.* First cut off the knuckle bone & simmer in the vegetable water to make some good stock. Roast for about 2 hours at No 2 gas (325°F) No need to baste. The long slow cooking will make the meat very tender, cook the vegetables and get out a lot of the surplus fat. Dish the meat, take out the vegetables with a slotted spoon, pour off the fat for use later and make gravy in the tin with the strong stock. To carve, the trick is to turn the joint upside down

*good sprinkled with rosemary

that is, with the crisp skin underneath. Hold the knife horizontally and cut slices flat from all over this side. (That is the underside which is now on top.)

Now there will be a good cut of cold lamb. To get this turn the meat over and carve from the sides. A good salad for lamb is made from chopped cucumber, mint, shredded raw cabbage, chives and salad cream. The beetroot salad on p. 12 also goes well. So do hot potatoes steamed in their skins, or more extravagant baked jacket potatoes.

On another day slices can be enjoyed in a small buttered oven dish interleaved with the cucumber sauce on p. 24 or onion sauce.

Onion Sauce. Chop a small onion and simmer in a little water for 10 minutes. Smooth a dessertspoonful of plain flour in a little milk. Add to the hot onion mixture and simmer for 5 minutes. Add a knob of butter or lamb fat, salt & pepper & pour over the slices of meat. Bake for 20 mins

Lamb needs:
Mint Rosemary. Cucumber, Onion

and red currant jelly.

The rest of the meat should be taken from the bone and kept in polythene bags in the freezer part of the fridge. Use the bones to make stock.

Mutton broth.

Fry a small chopped onion in lamb fat. Add lamb stock — about ½ pint. Add a finely chopped carrot. Taste for salt and pepper. Add a tablespoon of quick porridge oats, and a tablespoon of chopped lamb. A sweet red pepper adds to the flavour. Season with a teaspoon of mint sauce & a teaspoon of red currant jelly. Cooking time 20 minutes. Traditionally pearl barley was used instead of porridge. It does taste good but takes about 2 hrs and you need more stock as the longer cooking will reduce the broth.

Fillet Steak "Maître d'hôtel."

1 fillet steak — about 6 oz. 1 dessertspoonful each of butter, lemon juice and French mustard. Chopped parsley. Seethe the butter, lemon and mustard in a dry pan — rub with butter paper first to prevent sticking. Lay the meat in and press into the heat with a slice. Turn and repeat. About 1 minute each side will produce a rare but hot steak. Cheat and serve it with crisps and a good green salad. Sprinkle with parsley. This is the quickest dish I know!

Mushrooms are versatile:

Soup: ½ a chopped onion. 1oz mushrooms sliced. ¼pt chicken stock. ¼pt milk. A tablespoon red wine. Salt and pepper.

Cook onion in butter with the roughly chopped mushroom stalks until the onion is transparent. Add the wine (cider will do) and reduce by half, then add the stock and simmer for 10 minutes. Liquidise until very smooth. Add the milk, and the sliced mushroom, which is much better if tossed briefly in butter and flambé'd in a spoonful of brandy or sherry, taste and season. Bring to the boil and serve immediately. For perfection keep one mushroom cap back, chop it, put it into a spoonful of cream and add when the soup is in the plate.

Duxelle is made of equal quantities of shallots and mushrooms, both chopped fine. Onion may be used but has not the finesse. Use a knob of butter and soften the onion, add the mushrooms and cover. Simmer for

10 minutes. Chopped parsley may be added.
    Duxelle as a garnish to a fried slice of pork, veal or liver raises the dish to a new level.

Pumpkin.   This can be bought in slices, when in season. It will make a good soup and a delicious pudding.
    Peel, seed and cut up roughly and boil in salted water until tender – about 10 minutes.

Soup. Soften ½ a chopped onion in a dessertspoonful of butter and a pinch of curry powder. Stir for 3 minutes. Now blend the onion, half the pumpkin and ¼ pt chicken stock in the liquidiser. Bring to the boil and thin with cream or milk.

Pumpkin Ramekin.   Butter a ramekin. Beat an egg and mix with the rest of the cooked, sieved pumpkin. Add a pinch of mixed spice and a few sultanas and bake at No 4 until the egg is set. Sprinkle with sugar and pour on a little cream. A little brandy may be mixed with the spice.

Moules Marinières

½ pt mussels* Open these the french way. Scrub the mussels very clean cutting away any beard. Put them in a saucepan with a coffee cup of white wine or cider. 1 shallot (or some onion) cut very fine. 2 chopped parsley stems (keep the leaves for garnishing) a piece of bay leaf, a few leaves of thyme, black pepper and a knob of butter. Simmer. The mussels will open in moments.

Strain the juice through muslin (nylon stockings will do!). Simmer and reduce by half.

Arrange the mussels in a warm soup plate. Pour over the juice and sprinkle with chopped parsley.

A good starter to a simple meal is a mussel

*NB. Discard any mussels which are open before cooking or fail to open after cooking

cocktail.

Open the mussels as in the previous recipe but reduce the juice until it is just a moist patch at the bottom of the pan. Do not "forget" it as retribution is instantaneous! Squeeze in a blob of tomato paste, add a dessertspoonful of cream and another of mayonnaise. Squeeze a little lemon juice and a teaspoon of brandy or sherry on to the shelled mussels arranged in a glass and pour the sauce over them. Use a wedge of lemon as a garnish.

In Summer this cocktail tastes better if it is chilled.

Scampi Thermidor.

¼ lb scampi tossed in 1 oz bubbling butter.

1 gill of very thick, creamy, well seasoned Béchamel Sauce. (This is an ordinary white sauce of flour, butter & milk. The difference is that the milk is first brought to the boil and is flavoured with a little onion, celery, carrot and herbs. This hot milk is then left for at least ½ a hour for the flavours to infuse). ¼ pint of white wine reduced with a chopped shallot and a sprig of tarragon and parsley. 1 teaspoon of French mustard. Put the scampi, Béchamel, the very reduced wine (about a tablespoonful) and the mustard in a saucepan. Heat through. Pour into scallop shells,

sprinkle with grated cheese and flash under the grill. The classic Thermidor is made with lobster but any shell fish may be used. For those, who live alone, scampi is a good alternative.

    When you are making Béchamel sauce it is a good idea to make a pint using 2oz flour & 2oz butter. Put the onion, carrot, celery and herbs into the cold milk to extract the maximum flavour. When it has boiled leave to infuse. Make a roux with the butter & flour & season with sea salt and freshly milled black pepper. Use the amount you need. Add cream to improve the dish of the day. The rest of the sauce can be kept in a screw topped jar in the fridge for some time and will make some very good "instant" sauces.

Fish Pie.

    A good fish pie can be made quickly using 2oz smoked fish (cod, haddock or whiting.) and 2oz white fish (halibut, cod, haddock or similar). Cut the fish from the skin and remove any bones. Layer the mixed fishes in a greased pie dish with slices of mushrooms and a dusting of chives and parsley. Pour over a little white sauce (perhaps you have Béchamel in the fridge!) Otherwise make a sauce of ½ milk and ½ white wine or cider thickened with beurre manié

Top with mashed potato or pastry and bake for about 30 minutes.   A few prawns added to the mixture turn this dish into something special!

Fish is particularly good for solitary eaters and one of the things which is sold readily in small quantities. A fresh Cod steak Portuguaise makes a pleasant change. Take a tomato, a very small onion finely sliced and if liked a slice or two of sweet pepper.

Brush a stainless steel dish with oil — or rub with a butter paper and lay the steak on it. Grill for about 3 minutes and turn. Brush the turned side with oil and sprinkle with the slices of tomato, onion & sweet pepper. Season with freshly milled black pepper and sea salt. Grill for about 10 more minutes lowering the heat if the garnish is becoming too tanned.

Recently I enjoyed this dish with potatoes and Jerusalem artichokes cooked together. The vegetable took 20 minutes to cook and was started off just before grilling the fish.   A peeled potato cut small and a semi peeled Jerusalem artichoke were cooked together just covered with water. When the fish was nearly done the potato and artichoke were strained (I kept the water for a soup next day) and mashed with butter, then spooned on to the stainless steel dish.   The remark about semi-peeled artichoke refers to their diabolical skins which are knobbly, pitted and impossible.   As long as they are scrubbed a bit of peel couldn't matter less.   I comfort myself by thinking of all the vitamins and mineral salts which lie just under the skin and which are often wasted by thick peeling!

Trout with Fennel

I use the British fennel which grows weedlike in our garden.   The fish must be gutted and wiped clean inside.*   A handful of fresh bread crumbs and a teaspoon of butter are mixed with a little of the feathery fennel, salt and pepper.   Stuff the trout. Butter a chafing dish and lay the trout in.   Sprinkle with more chopped fennel and a little salt and pepper. Pour over a tablespoon of cream and cook at Gas No 4 for about 20 minutes.   Good with mashed potatoes and a wedge of lemon.

Kidneys as a main dish.

1 or 2 lamb's kidneys. Peel and wash well. Cut in half - but not quite - and flatten them. Dust with seasoned flour (plain flour, salt, pepper and if liked some herbs - a little fresh chopped mint is good)[p.54] Cut up a rasher of bacon and fry briefly. Add a little butter and seal the kidneys in this turning them once. This takes about one minute. Add a very finely chopped piece of onion, a mushroom cut into thin slices and stir for a few moments. Finally pour in a tablespoonful of wine, sherry or cider. (I like dry sherry best). Stir briefly, add a dessertspoonful of cream or top of the milk and enjoy with some type of potato or wholemeal toast. A good vegetable with this dish is a chicon of chicory cut into 4 lengthways and fried in butter or bacon fat.

Chicken and Parsley Soup.

This is a by-product of the boiled chicken with parsley sauce (p.7). If there is even a tablespoon of the sauce left over mix it with a cup of chicken stock, a teaspoonful of beurre manié (p.20), a tablespoonful of cream or top of the milk and some more chopped parsley.

If in extravagant mood use half white wine and half stock. It is a delightful soup.

Empanadinia of Prawns. (A Portuguese recipe).

Cut thinly rolled out short crust pastry into rings about 3" in diameter. Use 2 oz peeled prawns for a portion. Make a small amount of white sauce (or resort to the jar in the fridge p.33) about 1 coffee cup of milk and a heaped teaspoonful of beurre manié. If the prawns weep as they thaw this juice adds flavour to the sauce. Flavour with freshly grated nutmeg, sea salt and black pepper. Add the prawns when the sauce has cooled. Put little heaps of the mixture on to the pastry rounds, brush the edges with water, fold over and seal well. If left in the fridge for a time this really makes the joints set. Fry in very hot oil for about 5 minutes. If using a shallow pan turn after 2½ minutes.

These are good with a glass of white wine and a salad of sliced cucumber, sliced raw courgettes and cubes of melon. A wedge of lemon completes the dish.

Quail.

These little birds are delicious. It always amuses me to think they were part of the flesh pots of Egypt which kept the children of Israel havering for so long.

In a good deep frying pan, which will take a well fitting lid, melt a teaspoonful of butter. Sprinkle in a few sliced mushrooms and a very little finely chopped onion. Sprinkle sparingly with mixed sweet herbs. Fry the quail, or quails, all over, then pour in a coffee cup of red or white wine or cider. (I prefer the red wine). Cover closely and simmer for about 15 more minutes. Good eaten with any green vegetable (brussels sprouts are excellent) and old fashioned mashed potatoes or rice.

If liked a little finely cut streaky bacon may be used with the butter and mushrooms. One quail is enough but two are better ~ and fingers should be used to get your money's worth from them!

Mince with a difference.

¼ lb minced beef.   1 clove garlic, crushed.
1 level dessertspoon plain flour (wholemeal is best).
1 level dessertspoon quick oats. Salt, pepper and a
desertspoon of milk.   1 teaspoon of made mustard.
Mix together and make 2 thick rissoles. One may
be stored in the ice compartment of the fridge for use on
another occasion.   Grease a fire proof dish. Put
in the rissole(s) and grill for about 5 minutes on each
side.   While this is cooking poach an egg
so that it is slightly runny in the centre. Put the
egg on top of the rissole and use it as gravy. Serve
with a good crisp winter salad of cole slaw, chicory
and celery.   I prefer wholemeal toast to potato
or rice with this dish.

Devilled Chicken Legs.
    Make a marinade of 1 dessertspoon olive oil.
                    1 " wine vinegar or lemon juice.
   1 teaspoon curry powder. Dash of Worcestershire sauce.
Cut the leg(s) with a very sharp knife in a criss

cross pattern and turn in the marinade. Leave it or them in the fridge to soak and turn over often when you are passing. Boil a coffee cupful of rice in 2½ times the amount of water with a little chopped onion, carrot and celery. While this is cooking fry the chicken in the marinade turning frequently. The marinade will gradually evaporate and the chicken should be cooked in about 20 minutes. Add a teaspoon of tomato purée to the rice and stir very gently until the last of the water is gone. Serve the leg(s) and vegetable with chutney and a tomato and basil salad.

For the salad peel the tomatoes (in boiling water first) and sprinkle the slices with French dressing, fresh basil or parsley.

Tagliatelle Verdi with Egg, Vegetables & Cheese.
This is one of my favourite supper dishes. Any vegetables may be used but one of the best results come from a mixture of: sliced onion, sliced leek, (cut in thin rounds), courgette in thin rings, mushrooms in thin slices, green or red pepper cut fine, a tiny piece of chopped fresh ginger, a coffeespoon of mixed sweet herbs.
The tagliatelle is packed in round handfuls. 3 or 4 of these make a good serving. Boil in

plenty of fast moving salted water for about 12 mins. While this is cooking stir fry the vegetables in a tablespoonful of olive oil. They take about 5 minutes.

Strain the pasta and return to the pot. Add all the vegetables and stir. Re-heat briefly. Take off the heat and break in a raw egg. The heat from the cooking will turn this into an attractive creamy glaze. Mix well and dish into a warm soup plate. (I heat this with the water I strain from the pasta). Sprinkle generously with grated cheese. This dish only takes 15 minutes to achieve if you use boiling water from an electric kettle!

Most regional dishes are perfectly balanced diet-wise ~ protein, carbohydrate, vitamins etc. If cooking for more than one use an egg for each person. Spaghetti, macaroni or other pasta may be used with equal success.

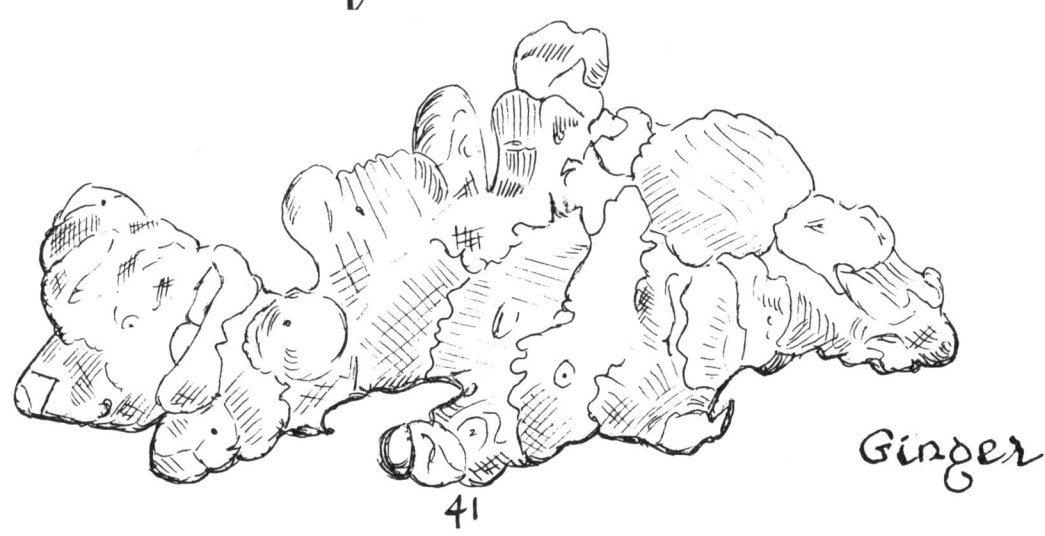

Ginger

Lamb Chops à l'Italienne

Dip the chop(s) into beaten egg and dry in breadcrumbs. If it does not stick very well, leave for a time and repeat. Boil a portion of spaghetti in boiling salted water for about 12 minutes. While this is cooking fry the chops in deep fat for 10 minutes or in shallow fat a little longer turning half way through the cooking.

Make a garlicky tomato sauce:

1 clove garlic, crushed, ½ a chopped onion & a tablespoon tomato paste. Fry together. Add a coffee cup of wine or cider. Simmer until thick. Fish out the garlic. Strain the pasta & place on a hot plate, top with the chop(s) and pour over the sauce. If the three bits of cooking are done to-gether this dish should be ready in 20 minutes. If possible it is a good thing to egg & breadcrumb the chops earlier and leave them to "set" in the fridge.

Brown Rice is a better flavour than the ordinary but it does take 40 minutes to cook. I cook about ½ lb at a time (raw weight) I brush a heavy small pot with oil. Wash & strain the rice & cover it with twice (generous) the amount of water. Add Sea Salt. Bring to the boil. Reduce heat & put on the lid. After about 20 minutes the water will have evaporated. Add a tablespoon more water, replace the lid and draw from the heat leaving only a bit of the saucepan in contact with the gas or electricity. When it is tender it can be kept in the fridge in a covered pot and used when wanted "instantly." It will fry hot in seconds, steam hot with the addition of a tablespoon of water or stock in the time it takes the fluid to boil or it will make an interesting ingredient for a salad.

Skate with Black Butter.

Buy a wing of skate. Wash well, dry and simmer in chicken stock. When tender, about 5 minutes, put on a hot plate and make the black butter. A good knob of butter should be cooked in a tiny pan until it starts to colour — have a care, you want it brown and it will quickly become too black! — add a squeeze of lemon juice. Pour over the fish and sprinkle with fresh chopped parsley.

Skate Soup.

Fry a tiny, chopped onion, in a knob of butter for 5 minutes. Add a good teaspoon of beurre manié (p.20) and the chicken stock the skate was cooked in. If necessary add a bit more chicken stock and/or wine or cider. Simmer for about 10 minutes. Season with sea salt and freshly milled black pepper. Add a tablespoon of cream or yogurt and serve with wholemeal toast.

Quick Tomato Soup.

Use a small tin Italian peeled tomatoes. Fry half a chopped onion in a little butter. Add the tomatoes & a coffee cupful of chicken stock. Season with sea salt and freshly ground black pepper, oregano and a coffee spoonful of sugar. Bring to the boil. Either sieve or liquidise.

Jambon Sauce Madère.

Cut two slices of ham into 3 or 4 pieces. Make a sauce of a knob of butter, 1 peeled & chopped tomato, beurre manié (p.20) about 1 good teaspoonful, salt, pepper, basil and a tablespoonful of Madeira wine or sweet sherry.

Butter a fireproof dish, layer the ham & sauce and cook briefly ~ it just needs to come to the boil ~

about 10 minutes in a medium oven (Gas mark 3).
This is good with new potatoes and spinach.

Avocado.
Use one half as 'Mbaraki' salad.
This is a dessertspoonful of mayonnaise, in which you have put a similar quantity of shredded raw leek, grated raw carrot and some cashew nuts.
Place this mixture in the cavity left by the stone.

Iced Avocado Soup. (No cooking)
Whisk up the other half with lemon juice, seasoning and enough chicken stock to make it liquid. Add a little cream or top of the milk. Chill. Rub a soup bowl with a clove of garlic. Pour in the soup & top with a little more cream that is sprinkled with chopped chives.

Vegetable Bake. 1 potato. 1 onion, 1 carrot. Stick of celery. 1 Jerusalem artichoke.
Cut the vegetables into rings and cubes. Toss them in seasoned flour (p. 54). Layer them in a small buttered casserole sprinkling with salt and pepper. Pour in enough boiling water not quite to cover them and finish with a layer of sliced potato

Put the lid on and bake for an hour. Take off the lid for the last 20 minutes, brush with melted butter and wait for the glorious sunset!

This is a good dish to put at the bottom of the oven when you are feeling that Sunday morning roast meat persuasion.

Crab is much cheaper than Lobster and makes a good: à l'Américaine.

Butter a scallop shell or a ramekin dish. Take 2 tablespoons of béchamel sauce (p. 33) and add a teaspoonful of brandy or sherry and half the amount of French mustard. Add the brown meat and heat. Toss in the white meat ~ about a heaped dessertspoon full of each colour and pour into the shell or dish. Sprinkle with fresh breadcrumbs and chopped parsley. Dot with butter and leave under the grill just long enough to make sure it is really hot. Overcooked crabmeat becomes strong and unpalatable.

It is easy to buy frozen crab meat. Served as Dressed crab it can be ready almost "instantly". Mix the white meat with a teaspoonful of mayonnaise, a similar quantity of brandy and a dash of cayenne pepper. Mix the brown with a teaspoonful of white wine vinegar, cayenne and a handful of fresh brown breadcrumbs. Tradition serves dressed crab with brown bread and butter and the heart of a lettuce.

Crab Rumble Tumble will finish the rest of the crab meat up if you purchased, originally, ½ lb.
Melt a knob of butter and fry the brown meat. Scramble in one egg and season with sea salt and cayenne pepper. Toss in the white meat for a few seconds. Serve on hot buttered toast. Very quick and very good.

Scallops "Billingsgate".

2 large scallops make an adequate serving. Soak them in cold water for half an hour.* This relaxes them and makes them tender.   *or longer.

Strain, dry and dust them with seasoned flour.

Grill 2 rashers of streaky bacon and place on a hot plate in a very low oven. Pour the bacon fat into a frying pan and cook the scallops ~ about 1~2 mins each side.   Eat the bacon and scallops together. The fish porters used to enjoy this dish with chips as a hearty breakfast when they knocked off work early in the morning.

Scallops with Fresh Haddock.

1 scallop. 2 oz fresh haddock. ¼ pt Béchamel (p33). salt and pepper to taste.

Slice the scallop and skin and cut small the fish.

Butter a fireproof dish. First layer a little of the sauce; then the scallop and fish and top with the rest of the sauce. Make a slice of wholemeal into crumbs and cover the dish. Dot with butter and sprinkle with grated cheese. Bake for about 20 minutes at Gas mark 4.

A Slice of Pork with Apple & Cider.

Persuade the butcher to cut a slice of pork from a leg. Bash it with a cleaver to flatten it. I put it between two chopping boards and stand on it! Dust with seasoned flour (p. 54) and brown briefly in a mixture of oil and butter – about a teaspoon of each. Turn & seal the other side. Take the meat out and fry half a chopped onion in the pan turning frequently. After 2 or 3 minutes add a sliced mushroom. Take out the onion and mushroom and place with the meat. Now add a coffee cup of cider to the pan and boil rapidly, stirring, until it is reduced by half.

Butter a shallow casserole and put in half the onion

and mushroom. Cover with the pork and the rest of the onion and mushroom. Sprinkle with sage. Cover with slices of raw Bramley apple and pour over the cider from the pan scraping it out well.

Bake at No 4 for 40 minutes*. White wine is as good, or better than the cider.   * It needs a good lid.
I like this dish with red cabbage.

Red Cabbage (A small one will keep in a polythene box in the fridge for a very long time)

Cut off a few slices. Cut up a cooking apple and ½ an onion. Fry the onion briefly in butter or olive oil. Add the shredded cabbage and the apple and add enough water mixed with cider or wine just to cover the vegetables. Add salt and cover closely. Simmer for about 30 minutes.

Tournedos flambé sur croute.

Buy a 6oz fillet steak. Trim it with a sharp knife (taking hardly anything off!) Give it a bash with a cleaver, or wide kitchen knife. Cut a slice of bread to the same shape. I put the meat on top of the bread and use it as a template.

Fry the bread golden brown and crisp in butter in a pan that never sticks (not a non-stick pan which spoils the flavour of the meat). Put the bread on a hot plate in a very low oven. Now fry the steak in the same pan. Use a bit more butter if it is at all dry. Fry quickly ~ 2 minutes each side for a medium rare tournedos.

Pour in a dessertspoonful of brandy or sherry and tip the pan up slightly so that it catches fire. Put the steak on to the fried bread. Warm a slice of tinned red pepper in the pan and use this to garnish the steak. Good with watercress salad and crisps or chips.

The pan juices finally are poured over the steak and the delicious taste of the brandy seems to concentrate in the bread.

The potatoes may be omitted as the bread takes their place. Fried chicory (p. 36) is an added delight. This is suitable for a celebration supper and easy to cook for two.

Boeuf Wellington.

A 4~6 oz Fillet steak.

First make the duxelle (p. 29). For one portion you need 1oz chopped mushrooms & 1oz chopped onion or better still shallots. 1 good knob of butter and one very small egg. Fry the onion in the butter (lid on, low heat). After 10 minutes stir in the mushrooms. Put a teaspoonful of the yolk of the egg and a similar quantity of milk on one side and scramble the rest of the egg into the onion/mushroom mixture. It goes a horrid grey colour - do not be dismayed.

Fry the steak briefly to seal it. Flavour the duxelle, egg mixture with salt and pepper.

Roll out about 3 oz pastry (flaky is considered correct, I prefer shortcrust. You may cheat and use frozen without a qualm). This should be twice as large as the steak. Put a layer of duxelle in the middle. Lay the steak on top. Cover and pack around with the rest of the duxelle. Draw up the pastry, moisten the edges and pinch them firmly together. Put it into the fridge and forget it for 24 hours. When you feel like enjoying this treat heat the oven to No 7, brush the pastry with the egg and milk glaze and bake for 35 minutes.

This is a splendid dish for entertaining a

deux. Twice the amount of steak and a soupçon more duxelle is enclosed in the Wellington and when serving the dish is sliced into two with a sharp knife.

Lamb with peppers. (Back to earth; with the best way I know of reheating roasted lamb [p.26])
 Cut an onion small and fry in a dessertspoonful of the mutton fat. Cut a green pepper small and lay on top of the onions. After 5 minutes cooking on very low heat in a well lidded pot, cut a tomato into rings and spread over the mixture. Then put a cupful of lamb on top — use the rough not so good looking pieces and cut them small with scissors — do not mince. Recover with the well fitting lid and simmer for at least 30 mins. The longer the better. Do not stir until ready to serve. Taste and add salt and pepper. Good eaten with rice and chutney.
 This is a South African recipe gleaned in the 1930s. In those days their mutton was of dubious quality and the long slow cooking made it edible. I cannot tell you how good it is with our delicious lamb and I defy anyone to know that it is reheated.

Gammon Steak.
 I like to soak gammon steak in fruit juice.

- whatever you have - apple is particularly good.

Then after half an hour (you can leave it in the fridge for longer if it is more convenient) lift it out, drain, dry with a little seasoned flour and grill very slowly.

Seasoned flour is so very useful to have ready. I keep ½ lb plain flour in a screw topped jar in the fridge. To this I add a heaped teaspoon of sea salt and about twenty twists of the black pepper mill. Then add a teaspoonful of sweet mixed herbs (parsley, thyme, marjoram, bayleaf) and shake well (lid on!) When you need a bit of flour for drying meat or fish it is ready "instantly".

In a small buttery pan fry a small quantity of chopped onion or shallot, add a dessertspoonful of the seasoned flour and when this is mixed well, gradually add the fruit juice the gammon was soaked in. Add a little made mustard and if necessary a touch of sugar. If already too sweet it can be retrieved with a teaspoonful of wine vinegar. Bring to the boil, simmer long enough to ensure that the flour no longer tastes raw and finally pour over the gammon.

Good with mashed potatoes and spinach.

Cheese and Semolina Souffle.

Memories of school cooking and sago and tapioca make us think semolina is the same sort of mush. But it isn't. It is the heart of the Durom wheat, very nutritious and very edible providing it is not mixed with milk and sugar in a pudding!

¾ oz Semolina (as supplied for making puddings)
¼ pt milk.   1 egg.   Salt, pepper, mustard, cayenne/or tobasco, worcestershire sauce or similar.
1 oz grated cheddar cheese.

Brush a small soufflé dish with oil. (I always keep a small stone jam jar on a saucer near the cooker. In it sits a small pastry brush and about a tablespoon of olive oil. I use it to brush fry pans, cooking tins, casseroles and the like. It obviates sticking and makes the washing up a pleasure instead of a chore. Also if you are worrying about calories, frying can be achieved in the very minimum of fat.)   Or you may rub it with a butter paper.   Put the oven on at No 4.

Bring the milk to the boil, sprinkle in the semolina and stir until thickish. (about 50 seconds). Take off the heat and break in the egg. Stir well. Add the seasonings and the cheese and pour and scrape into the prepared dish.

Cook for about 35 minutes.

I enjoy this with a mixture of root crops. Last time I used a little boiling water in a small closely cidded saucepan and to this I added half a cubed small potato, similar of Jerusalem artichoke, onion, carrot, celery and parsnip. (p. 24.)

These were exactly ready with the soufflé which takes a bit longer to cook than the 20 minutes the vegetables require. The vegetables were scrubbed and peeled (or not!) while the water was coming to the boil.

This water with a bare teaspoon of marmite and a tablespoon of sherry made a pseudo consommé & the strained vegetables with a knob of butter were delicious with the Soufflé.

Lobster Loaf. is one of my delights. If it is difficult to get a fresh lobster the dish can be made with scampi or prawns. You need a portion of long French loaf. Cut off about 6". Cut in half lengthways and scoop out the crumb leaving a bit each end.
Either use cooked, chopped lobster meat, or prawns, or if using scampi just toss these in butter to cook them. They are done when they curl back into shape.
Stuff the cavity of bread with the fish, plenty of soft butter, a squeeze of lemon juice and a dash of cayenne pepper.

Put back the lid. If the stuffing is proud it will

fill the roof too.   Tie in two places with string.
   Bake for 15 minutes at No 4.   This is delicious. The only drawback is the mess you get into when you eat it!   Like Deborah and her orange in Cranford I wonder if I, too, should resort to a hip bath suitably screened ~~~

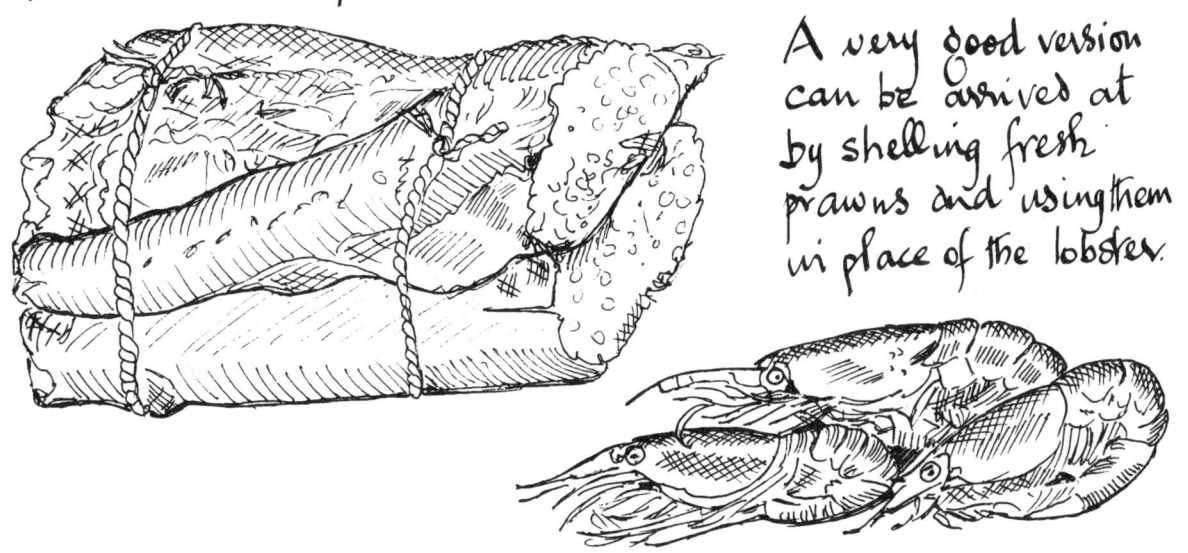

A very good version can be arrived at by shelling fresh prawns and using them in place of the lobster.

Escalope of Veal or Pork.
   The secret with an escalope is to bash it out until it is twice as big.   When it cooks it shrinks. If bashed it returns to its natural size ~ if not it tends to be a sad disappointment and a bit on the rubbery side in texture.
   If you have no cleaver, place between two chopping boards and mark time. This works wonders!

moisten the escalope on both sides in a saucer ful of marsala wine, sherry or vermouth. Then dry in seasoned flour (p. 54). Fry in a good knob of butter on gentle heat ~ about 3 minutes each side. Pour in a little cream & any alcohol left in the saucer.

An escalope of pork cut from the top of the leg can be treated the same way. Often it is easier to extract a suitable cut from the butcher.

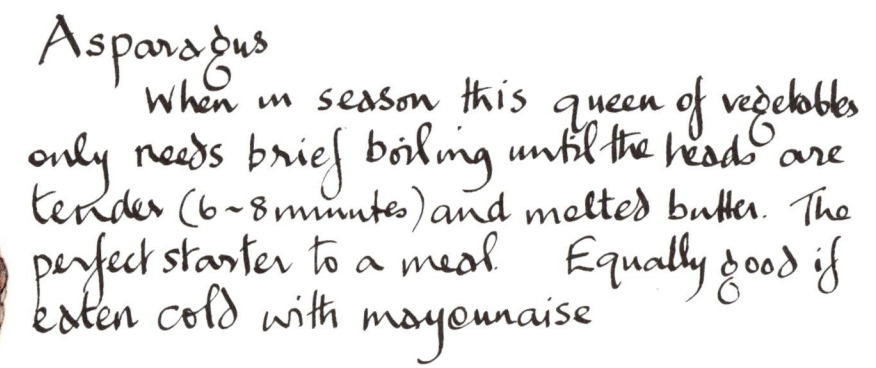

Asparagus

When in season this queen of vegetables only needs brief boiling until the heads are tender (6-8 minutes) and melted butter. The perfect starter to a meal. Equally good if eaten cold with mayonnaise

A Salmon Steak poached in white wine.

Put the salmon in a small pan just wide enough to hold it. Pour over a mixture of water, wine (or cider) salt, pepper, bayleaf, and a little onion. This should barely cover the fish. Cover with a well fitting lid and bring to the boil. Immediately reduce heat and simmer very gently for about 6 minutes. Put fish on a hot platter and reduce liquid, boiling rapidly until just one tablespoon is left.   Add a knob of butter and strain over the fish.

Excellent with plain boiled minted new potatoes and peas.   These can be cooked together in one pan — give the potatoes a 12 minute handicap, then add the peas.   If you start the potatoes off, then poach the salmon, the dish will be ready at the same time

Keep the pea & potato water to make:

Summer Soup.
   Pea & potato water.
   Mint. Chives.
   1 finely chopped onion
   A tablespoon of white wine
        or cider.

   Beurre manié.

Cook the onion in a small pot brushed with oil. Add the pea & potato water and the chopped fresh mint. Bring to the boil. Add the wine & thicken with beurre manié. (p.20).   I have just discovered an even easier way of making this friend of the cook.

Now can be bought in the Super markets is a pot called "Clover." It is made of dairy cream and tasteless vegetable oil. As a result it tastes like a creamy butter but spreads straight from the fridge. When beurre manié is made of clover and plain flour it is instantly mixable and once stored in the fridge is far easier to spoon out.

Clover is also quite the best and easiest way of making Sandwiches.

Petti di Pollo alla Valdestramo. (A very favourite dish)

1 chicken breast. (Frozen will do) Thaw overnight. Skin. Take out any bone and then flatten the breast between two boards and gently tread it flat.

Simmer the skin and bone with a piece of onion, carrot & celery in about ½ pint of water.

Dust the breast with seasoned flour (p.54) and fry in a dessertspoonful of butter very, very gently. About 3 or 4 minutes each side. Put the chicken on a stainless steel plate, cover with slices of raw mushroom and then very, very thin slices of a melting cheese. Our native cheddar is quite all right, though I doubt whether our E.E.C partners would agree~~~

Reduce the chicken stock to about a tablespoonful, and put this and a similar quantity of brandy or sherry into the buttery pan. Reduce a little and add a knob of butter.

While making the sauce grill the chicken until the cheese is melted and the chicken hot (about 5 mins) Pour over the sauce. I ate this today with new potatoes cooked with broad beans & chicory fried at the same time as the chicken. Apart from the earlier preparation and making the stock (which I did while washing up at breakfast time) the whole dish was ready in the time it took to boil the new potatoes. It was delicious!

Poussin. Sometimes it is possible to buy a poussin — a baby roasting chicken.

For the stuffing I use 1 slice wholemeal bread made into fresh crumbs, 1 rasher streaky bacon cut small with scissors, a tiny piece of chopped onion, or better still a shallot, a lot of chopped parsley, enough to turn the stuffing green, a little finely grated lemon zephyr, sea salt and black pepper, a little thyme and a good blob of soft butter. Mix and stuff the bird loosely — never cram stuffing into anything — else the bird will not cook properly and the juices will not mingle with the bread.

Brush with melted butter and roast at No 4 for 30 or 40 minutes. The bird is cooked when it is possible to put a pointed knife or a knitting pin between the body and the thigh bone and for the juice to run out clear (not pink.) If before you start on your stuffing you heat up the oven it is an opportunity to cook a baked jacket potato. By the time the bird is in the oven both it and the potato should be ready together.

All it needs is an attractive vegetable such as beans or broccoli or similar.

Most green vegetables take between 6 & 8 minutes after the water has come to the boil again.

French beans are often available out of season. They are very good just cooked in salted water and after straining have a knob of butter as a garnish.

Living alone a colander is far too big and a small sieve ~ about 6" in diameter is much more useful. I keep 2 ~ one for sieving flour and one for vegetables ~ otherwise a moist sieve

French Beans.

62

and flour makes an impenetrable mess! One of the things a wise cook only does once ~ ~ ~

A Belgian way of cooking French beans is instead of the butter to cook a finely chopped piece of streaky bacon until crisp and the fat runs. Then tip the lot over the beans. This would go very well with the poussin.

Runner Beans are so very good because we have to wait for them and then they do not last long.
    When fresh from the garden they are just as good broken into 1" lengths as thinly sliced.
    They make a delicious salad if you cook too many (on purpose).
    Mix them with chopped ham, a French dressing and some chopped chives and parsley.

Brussels Sprouts — the small ones are best; taste much better cooked with equal quantities of salt and sugar in the boiling water. In 6-8 minutes they are crisp, nutty and delicious.

Cabbage with Mace or Nutmeg.
Cabbage, shredded, and cooked very quickly in salted, boiling water, strained dry and topped with a knob of butter is ready in about 4 minutes. It is good with Pork or Ham with an added dash of mace or freshly grated nutmeg. Mace is the outer covering and more difficult to buy in the blade form. Powdered mace is disappointing. A whole nutmeg is easy to buy and the flavours are similar.

Potatoes.
Many of the dishes described lend themselves to sauté or fried potatoes.
When boiling potatoes always cook too many so that they are ready in the fridge for "instant" conversion into many varieties:

Almost Chips. Cut the cold potato into chip shaped pieces. Fry in shallow fat and turn. This is a good way of achieving "chips" without having to get a deep pot of oil hot & the attendant smell.

Santé or fried potatoes.
   Slice the potato and fry slowly in butter, oil or bacon fat until crisp and golden. Turn once.

Lyonnaise potatoes.
   Cut an onion small and fry gently until soft and transparent. Add thinly sliced potato and fry, turning frequently until all the onions and potatoes are golden brown. Sprinkle with salt, pepper and parsley or thyme.

Mashed potatoes.   My favourite aunt who is 88 makes the best mashed potatoes I know. I think she is heavy handed with the butter & top of the milk. She always makes too much. She then either reheats in a low oven or makes potato cakes with the addition of a very small egg, shapes them, rolls them in seasoned flour and fries them gently in dripping or butter.

Cauliflower is versatile. It will keep well in the polythene containers in the fridge and portions can be cut off with a sharp pointed knife.

   It makes a good salad raw. Cut the florets small and the stems even smaller. Dress with mayonnaise and chives.

It is good just boiled in salted water, a knob of butter added after straining. The water is too strong and, regretfully, is better tipped down the sink.

Covered with cheese sauce and browned in the oven it is a supper dish on its own.

Also the final piece will make a Russian Salad. Cut a young carrot into rings, or an old one into cubes and simmer for 8 minutes. Add the florets of cauliflower cut small and any stem cut even smaller and simmer for 5 minutes; finally add a tablespoonful of frozen peas and cook for another 4 minutes by which time all the vegetables should be tender but not overcooked. Strain and keep the water. Dress the salad with mayonnaise and chopped chives and parsley while still hot. Mix well and chill. Very good with hot new potatoes and cold meat. In the winter a small piece of raw onion forced through a garlic press will take the place of the chives.

The water makes the basis of a vegetable soup. It is

excellent as a "thinner" for a concentrated commercial soup or a dry packet mix.

Sugar Peas (Mange Tout) are so easy to cook. A few minutes in salted, boiling water and a knob of butter and they are ready. Their water is a bonus that should never be wasted. I like it chilled mixed with tomato juice & a dash of lemon as a thirst quencher. It also makes wonderful pea soup with the addition of a handful of peas, beurre manié, a sprig of chopped mint and a spoonful of top of the milk or cream. No salt, because it is already in the water.

They can also be cooked on a bed of half fried onions, the outer, shredded leaves of a lettuce, a tight fitting lid and a little patience. It spoils their colour but they taste wonderful!

Purple Sprouting Broccoli.
This cooks in 6-8 mins in boiling salted water. It can be eaten like asparagus with melted butter, used as a vegetable with almost

61

any meat or poultry dish, or if you cook too much the extra pieces are a delicious salad dipped into French dressing (sauce vinaigrette).

French Dressing (p 8.)

Cauliflower florets and finely chopped stems~

A young Marrow can be used many ways

My favourite is a slice of young marrow, cubed, skin pips and all. It must be very young. A spoonful of chopped fried onion, a tomato peeled and sliced, salt, pepper and the marrow on top. Cover well and simmer for about 15 minutes.

A section about 1½" thick can be cut off, the seeds are then pushed out and the cavity filled with sausage meat seasoned with mixed herbs, a sliced mushroom, a very little finely chopped onion. Place in a buttered pie dishlet, cover with bacon and bake gently for about 30 minutes.

Italians cut the slices fine, dip them in batter and fry in fat or oil for about 5 minutes.

If cubed and boiled for about 2 minutes, when cool it can be dressed with yogurt and chives.

Celery will keep in the fridge for a long time. I always have a head on the go. Outer stems can be chopped and boiled; used for flavouring stock; added to mixed root crop brews. Make 2" lengths to fill with cream cheese and use as a pre supper appetiser with an aperitif. The outer stems blanched and stewed in gravy can be "forgotten" in the oven with a butter paper to keep them from drying up in the shelf underneath a roast. The heart can be eaten with cheese. The versatility is endless.

Spinach will cook in seconds. Wash it well & strain. Then cook it gently in a pan brushed with oil. Add a very little salt. Cover closely and it will be done in about 4 minutes.

An extra nice Winter vegetable is Swedes & Turnips cooked together with added watercress and cream. Do make too much as it will warm up without tasting reheated. Cut a white turnip and a small Swede into dice. They need to be fairly thickly peeled. Simmer until tender, strain, then add a tablespoonful of chopped watercress (stems & all) and a tablespoonful of cream. Add sea salt and freshly ground black pepper to taste. Very good served with pork or ham.

Although frozen chicken portions are all right they

are far more expensive than a whole chicken.

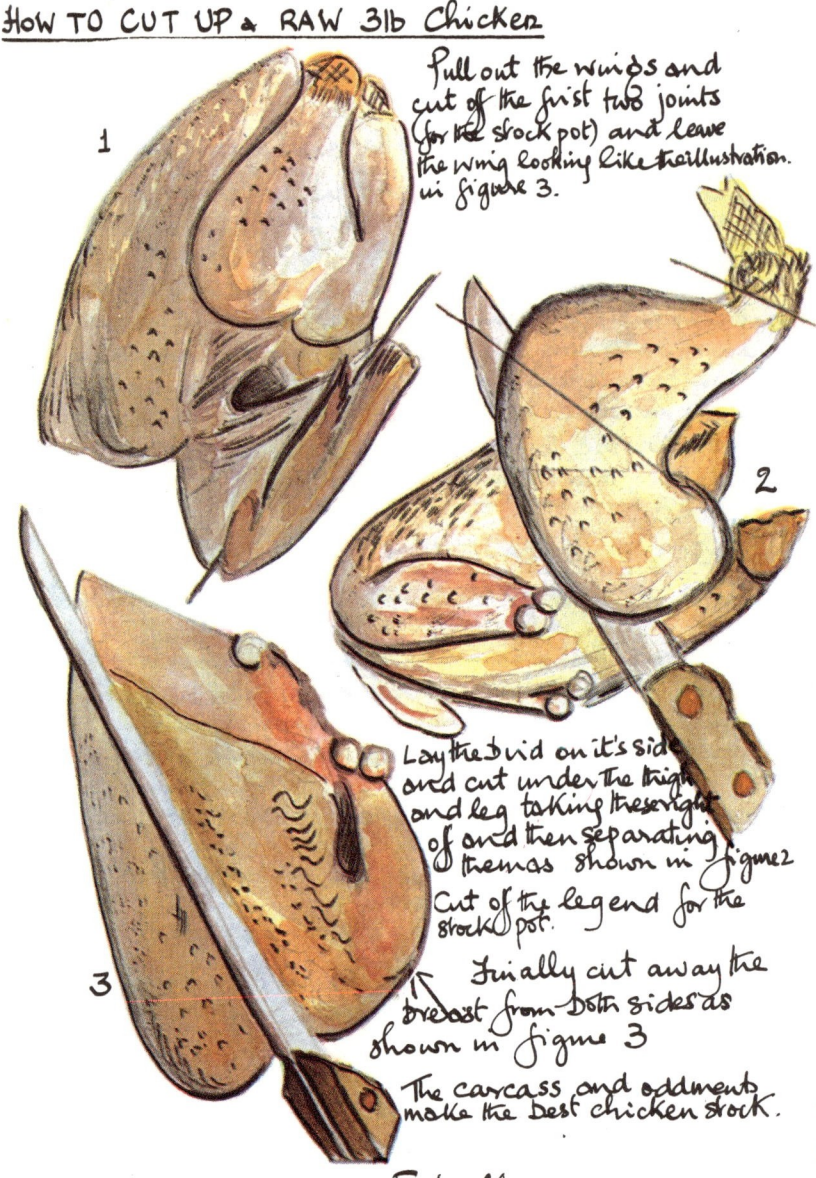

HOW TO CUT UP A RAW 3lb Chicken

1. Pull out the wings and cut of the first two joints (for the stock pot) and leave the wing looking like the illustration in figure 3.

2. Lay the bird on it's side and cut under the thigh and leg taking the weight of and then separating them as shown in figure 2. Cut of the leg end for the stock pot.

3. Finally cut away the breast from both sides as shown in figure 3.

The carcass and oddments make the best chicken stock.

Once you have tackled a bird this way you will find it quite easy.

You can use a breast for Petits di Pollo alla Valdestram (p.60) and the legs for the Devilled dish on p.39. The thighs (one makes an ample portion) are my favourite cut. They can be fried in butter very slowly, without benefit of breadcrumbs.

Turn once. Pour in a little dry white vermouth and a coffee cup of chicken stock. Cover and simmer until tender.

Finally thicken with beurre manié and add a spoonful of cream. Serve on top of a bed of rice and pour all the sauce over. If you are making use of cooked rice it can be reheated in the sauce. Eat with a good crisp salad.

The other breast and thigh can be wrapped and frozen for future use. I think you will find this a real economy and the chicken stock from the raw bones quite excellent for many uses.

Liver with onions.

Liver tends to become tough with cooking. An easy way is to cook it with onions.

Chop a small onion fine and cook in a lidded frying pan with a knob of butter. When the onion is transparent but not coloured, add the liver (dried in seasoned flour (p.54)). One or two slices of lamb's liver makes a good portion. Calves liver is very difficult to come by and ox is too strong. Pig's liver is just about as good as lamb's.

Cover and cook very, very slowly for about 5 minutes. Then turn and give the other side about 2 minutes. Dish the liver, brown the onions briefly over a high heat, stirring all the time and it is ready.

If you like it with gravy put a spoonful of beurre manié into the pan and add a little stock or vegetable water. A very little marmite will flavour & colour the gravy.

Beefburgers.   This is a recipe, using minced beef, which comes from the U.S.A.

8 oz mince will make 4 burgers. These can be frozen.
1 egg, salt, pepper and a teaspoonful of made mustard.
1 cup quick porridge oats.
1 tablespoonful of tomato ketchup.
A dash of tabasco or Worcestershire sauce.

Break the egg into the centre of the mince. Add all the other ingredients and mix well. Form into four or 6 burgers.

They should be grilled and served with a sharp sauce such as barbecue. Do not overcook. about 8 mins.

Claret Balls.   (A Greek recipe)
½ lb lean minced beef.
½ small onion chopped very fine. (the other is used later).
½ slice wholemeal bread soaked in claret. (squeeze dry).
½ cup cooked rice. (Must be dry).

Mix all together. Add salt, pepper & a very small egg. Form into about 10 meat balls. Dry in seasoned flour (p.54) and fry in olive oil briefly to seal. Take out.

Fry the other half of the chopped onion in the oily pan. If necessary add a bit more oil. When the onion is tender add a dessertspoonful of tomato purée, a coffee spoon of brown sugar, the claret squeezed from the bread and a half sherry glass more claret. Put the meat balls back and cook very slowly until the meat tastes cooked (about 20 minutes). Add a little butter and garnish with slices of hard boiled egg.

The balls are good hot with a green vegetable and new potatoes. They are excellent cold with a crisp salad and potato mayonnaise.

This is a surprisingly delicious dish.

Torta Pasqualina. (A Genoese recipe).

Butter, Spinach, Onion, Curd cheese, Eggs, pastry. Fry ½ chopped onion in ½ oz butter until transparent, add a handful of washed spinach and cook with a lid on until just tender. Chop well, season with salt, pepper and grated nutmeg. Add a handful of curd or cottage cheese, extract as much liquid as possible from the mixture. Spread in a very small, buttered, oven dishlet. Make 2 hollows and break an egg in each. Cover with pastry and bake at NO 7 for 35 minutes when the eggs should be set and the pastry crisp.

Avgolemono. (A Greek recipe).

1 egg. 1 lemon. ½ cup cooked rice. 1pt of chicken stock. Salt & pepper.

(Wedges of lemon are easier to squeeze cut this way).

Simmer the cooked rice (if necessary start with raw) in the stock until the grains are overcooked. Heat and add the lemon juice.

Beat the egg in a warm soup bowl, first the white & then the yolk. Now add the soup a spoonful at a time beating all the while. Serve at once.

This is an interesting different taste and very suitable in summer as a starter to a cold luncheon.

Celery, Apple & Tomato Soup.

This soup should be a delicate rose pink and not too thick; an interesting variation on the more ordinary celery soup.

2 oz chopped outside stalks of celery.
½ cooking apple, chopped. 1 peeled tomato.
1 small chopped onion. 1 small chopped potato.
½ pt chicken stock. ½ pt milk. 1 oz butter.

Soften the onion, celery & potato gently in the butter but do not brown. Add apple, tomato, salt, pepper & stock. Simmer until the celery is tender, liquidise & sieve. This gets rid of the celery strings & the tomato pips.

Add milk and re-heat, checking the seasoning. Basil (especially fresh) improves the flavour. (enough for twice).

Almond Soup.

2 oz ground almonds.
1 oz diced ham. 1 oz chopped celery.
1 oz chopped onion. ½ oz butter.
1 pt chicken stock. 1 clove. Pinch of mace.
½ bay leaf, basil, salt, pepper, dash of sherry.

Melt butter and gently cook onion, celery, ham and then add stock & clove, mace, bay leaf, basil and seasoning. Bring slowly to the boil and simmer for half an hour. Strain soup, pressing the juice out well and return to the pan. Stir in the almonds and **simmer** for about 10 minutes. Add the sherry and serve garnished with toasted flaked almonds.

To toast almonds spread out on a buttered cake tin and leave for a few minutes in a medium oven. They soon begin to colour. If you do quite a few and then keep them in an air tight container they can be used to garnish both sweet and savoury dishes.

Cream of Onion Soup

1 small onion, chopped. 1 celery stalk, chopped. 1 small sliced potato, (this thickens the soup). ½ oz butter, ¼ pt chicken stock. ¼ pt milk. Salt and pepper. Chives.

Sweat the onion and celery in the butter, add stock and potato and season well. Simmer for 15 minutes and then sieve or liquidise. Finally add enough milk to make a pleasing consistency. Heat. Garnish with cream and chopped chives. In hot weather this soup is good served iced. Often I have it hot one day and the rest chilled the next.

Carrot and Orange Soup. (Hot or iced)

¼ lb peeled and sliced carrots. 1 small onion. ½ oz butter. Pared rind of ½ orange. 1 sliver of lemon peel. Bay leaf, thyme, juice of ½ orange. Sea salt, black pepper. ¾ pt chicken stock. *

Sweat onion and carrots in the butter (lid on, low heat, for about 20 minutes. Add the stock, the fruit peel, bay leaf, thyme and seasoning. Simmer for 10 minutes. Liquidise, sieve, and add the orange juice. Either reheat or chill. * If a spicier flavour is liked add a teaspoon of curry powder when sweating the onions.

Watercress Soup.

½ bundle cress. 1 potato. 1 small onion. ¼ pt

milk and ¼pt water.   Salt, pepper, cream or yogurt. Reserve a spoonful of chopped watercress leaves. Roughly chop the stems and rest of the leaves, onion, unpeeled potato Simmer in the water until tender. Liquidise and sieve. Taste, season, reheat with the milk and serve with the reserved cress in a generous spoonful of cream or yogurt. This is the one soup which is better not made with stock.

Cucumber Soup.   (Hot or iced.)

½ onion, chopped. ¼ cucumber peeled and diced. Mint. ½ oz butter. ¼pt stock. ¼pt milk, cream or yogurt. Sweat onion in the butter, add cucumber, chopped mint, seasoning and stock. Simmer until tender. Liquidise and then add the milk. Either reheat or chill. Either way serve garnished with cream or yogurt & chopped mint.

Cheese Spread.

1 oz butter, 1 peeled tomato, 1 heaped teaspoon mustard. Sea salt, black pepper. Worcestershire sauce. Tablespoon of beer or cider.   Cook together until the tomato becomes a sauce.   Add ½ lb grated cheese. (Cheddar is best.) When the cheese is melted take off the heat and stir in 1 egg.

This can be stored in the fridge. Use it to cover toast and grill; for cheese sandwiches, or as an "instant" cheese sauce when combined with the

Bechamel recipe on page 33.

To make a Buck Rabbit grill the spread on toast and top with a poached egg.

Sole en goujeons.

Get the fishmonger to fillet a sole for you. Cut the fillets into small strips (scissors are best). Coat these in seasoned flour (p.54) dip into beaten egg, roll in dry breadcrumbs and deep fry.

Serve with tartare sauce. (p.15).
Once prepared the goujeons can be frozen in a polythene bag and used as & when required. They will keep in the ice making compartment of the fridge.

Madeira Egg.

¼ chopped onion cooked in butter, ½ oz flour, and ¼ pt of meat stock. Cook together and reduce a little. Now add a tablespoonful of madeira wine or sweet sherry and a tablespoonful of top of the milk. Season with salt and pepper. Simmer until the sauce has the consistency of thick cream. Skin and chop a tomato and add to the sauce.

Boil an egg for 5 minutes. Run under the cold tap. Peel. Place in a bowl and pour the sauce over.

Serve with hot buttered toast.

Lobster Oregano.

Boil a lobster for 8 minutes in a lot of salted boiling water. Split open while still hot. Place in a buttered baking dish. (The stomach sack in the head should be removed and any strips of the black back passage which runs through the centre of the body and is obvious when the fish is split in half.) Melt ½ oz butter with a dessertspoonful of olive oil. Add a teaspoonful of chopped parsley, basil, oregano, a tiny piece of garlic. Spread this mixture over the tails. Crack open the claws. Chop the meat. Mix with a tablespoon of fresh breadcrumbs and a teaspoon of parmesan. Spread on top of the tails. Dab with butter and bake at Gas mark 5 for 15 minutes.
You may use a cooked lobster but the reheating tends to make it tough.

Piperade.   (An ideal Television supper.)
  Butter, olive oil, a little onion, a rub of garlic, a peeled tomato and a slice or so of chopped sweet pepper.
Cook these ingredients together until a moist, tender muddle in the pan.   Season with salt and pepper. Make one or two slices of crisp wholemeal toast & stand upright to let the steam escape.
  Now scramble one or two eggs into the muddle.   Cook very quickly never ceasing to stir.
  Pour over the toast~

Belgian Fluffy Omelettes.
  The sweet omelette described on p.10 belongs to this brigade.   They are very quick to make, foolproof, light and delicious.
  They are best accompanied by rather "dry" flavourings.
  The secret is to separate the whites from the yolks.   2 eggs are better than one unless you have a very small appetite.   Whip the whites stiff. Add the yolks and whip briefly.
  Cook gently in a well buttered pan. Only one side is cooked. The inside is left fluffy.
  Season with a sprinkling of salt and pepper.

Here are some suggested fillings.

    Fines Herbes. Chopped parsley with an added sprinkle of dried herbs: thyme, marjoram, tarragon. Fresh chives are good just with the parsley.

Cheese. Grated and sprinkled generously.

Bacon. Cut small and fried crisp. In this case it is better to cook the omelette in the bacon fat.

Mushroom. Cook the sliced mushrooms briefly in butter in the omelette pan. Remove, cook the omelette. Sprinkle over.

In each case the omelette is folded in two and slipped on to a hot plate.

    If you would like the cheese version with a more substantial sauce, cook onion, tomato, sweet peppers salt, pepper and a spoonful of mixed herbs in a separate pan. When the omelette is dished, pour the sauce over the top.

Curry Sauce. If this is made in sufficient quantity it will keep in the fridge in a closed container for about a fortnight and seems to improve with maturity. Here are some basic ingredients. Do not fail to add and subtract as the spirit dictates:

    For about 1pt ~ 1½ pts use. 1 oz butter. 1 large onion, chopped. 1 cooking apple or rhubarb, chopped

How to chop an onion

Peel the onion down towards the root. Cut away the root.

Cut the onion in half lengthways and quickly place both halves face down on the chopping board.

Cut the half into five or six lengthways.

Now cut across at rightangles and you have a chopped onion and no crying.

Bromleys

1 tablespoon of dessicated cocoanut covered in water and brought to the boil for 2 minutes.
1 tablespoon curry powder
1 tablespoon Garam masala.
1 tablespoon fruit syrup or jam.
1 tablespoon sultanas.
A small piece fresh ginger, chopped. Cook the onion in the butter and then summer in all the other ingredients. Season with salt and pepper and then make up to a pint with freshly brewed Indian tea.

Once made this sauce will prove very useful.

Here are some ideas for its use:

Curried Lamb.
   Cut up a cupful of roasted lamb into small cubes. Simmer in a little sauce. Add a little fresh mint or mint sauce and it is ready.

Curried Fish.   Any white fish is suitable.
   Cut 4oz into cubes. Dip in a batter made of flour, salt and milk — about a dessertspoonful of seasoned flour (p.54) and enough milk to made a consistency like double cream.   Dip the fish in and fry for 1 minute in oil. Drain. Put into a hot dish and pour over some warm curry sauce.

Curried Prawns.
   Fry 4oz very briefly in butter. Add 2 tablespoons of sauce & re-heat. Have a care. Overcooked shellfish goes to rubber.

Always serve slices of tomato, banana, poppadums and mango chutney as a garnish and plain boiled rice.

Poppadum

83

Poppadums are easy to buy in good grocers. They need the briefest of time in boiling oil turning once. It is quite exciting to watch them expand!

Curried chicken.
    Can be made the same way as the lamb or you can use raw chicken cut small, sealed in butter and then simmered until tender in the sauce - about 20 minutes.

Curried Eggs.
    These do not even require rice as they are good served on hot buttered toast.
    Hard boil 2 eggs and cut each into four length ways. Briefly heat in enough sauce to cover them. Again sprinkle with banana, tomato and chutney.

Risotto. This can be made with long grain rice or with the brown rice (pre cooked see p. 42).
    It can be a vegetarian dish or liver, kidneys & garlic sausage may be used.
    Here is the vegetarian version first:
Fry a small chopped onion in ½ oz butter. Add some slices of chopped sweet pepper, a chopped tomato, parsley, marjoram, salt and pepper. Wash the rice well

(about 2 tablespoonsful) add to the brew and then pour in a large cupful of water, or stock. Pea water is particularly good.   Simmer until all the fluid is gone and the rice is tender. You can always add another spoonful of water if the rice is chewy. Cook with a lid on so that the rice is in the steam.   Add a knob of butter. Put into a flameproof dish, cover with grated cheese and flash under the grill until golden brown and bubbling.

For the Meat version I like to use the pre-cooked brown rice. Fry a chopped onion in butter, as before. Add a small cupful of slices of garlic sausage cut into 4, a rasher of bacon or a slice of ham, cut small, a kidney cut into cubes. Cook the meat with the onion, a small chopped sweet pepper and a chopped tomato. Season. When the vegetables are cooked (about 10 mins) add 3 tablespoonsful of cooked rice and just enough stock to moisten. Simmer, lidded for 5 minutes. Sprinkle with chopped parsley. If liked this version also, can be finished off with grated cheese, grilled.

Other meat is also suitable.   Tongue, chicken, pork and veal all make delicious risotto — either on their own, or mixed in various ways.   Liver and bacon are very tasty together. Use the herbs to go with the meat chosen: for instance sage with pork and rosemary with kidney

Smoked Herring.   This is one of my delights.
Buy Kipper fillets. Pull off the skin and soak in lemon juice for at least 1 hour. The juice of 1 lemon is ample for 4 fillets.

Then slice thinly and use like smoked Salmon. Either serve with brown bread & butter or make thin brown bread & butter sandwiches with a generous filling. Dust with cayenne.

Russian Eggs.
These are hard boiled eggs. Cut them in half lengthways and take out the yolk. Mix the yolks with anchovy fillets — about 1 fillet and a little oil mixed well together and then replaced in the white of the egg.

Russian Eggs & Smoked Herring fillets served together with heart of lettuce and brown bread and butter make a delicious Supper dish.

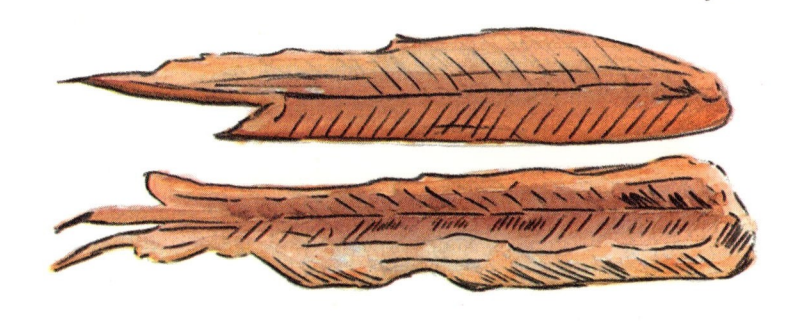

Now, I haven't said much about puddings. Living alone I am inclined to have a bowl of fresh fruit

However it is very useful to have an assortment of Petits Fours type mouthfuls in an airtight container & have a selection with coffee. Here are some suggestions. (If quite a lot of one variety is made at one time and then stored, quite soon plenty will be available!)

Almond paste. is made by mixing
    4oz ground almonds, 4oz icing sugar.
    white of 1 egg and a teaspoon of liquer or brandy.
Mix all together to form a stiff paste. This can be used to stuff dates (stoned) — prunes, soaked & stoned, and dried apricots, soaked. It can also be cut into little shapes.

Fudge.   Beat 1½oz cream cheese until light and fluffy. Add, gradually, 6oz icing sugar. Dissolve a level dessertspoonful of instant coffee in 1 teaspoon of boiling water. In this melt 1oz of plain chocolate.   Add to the cream cheese mixture. Now add 1oz of seeded raisins.

Line a tin with greaseproof paper and spread the mixture evenly. Score into shapes and place a nut or glacé fruit on top of each.   Chill and when very, very cold cut down through the score marks.

Cocoanut Ice. (Granny Wolfie's recipe).
   ½ grated fresh cocoanut. (The blue tits get the other)
   1lb cube sugar.   Knob of butter. 1 dessertspoonful of
   cream and a few drops of cochineal.

Take the cocoanut water and add enough water to make ¼pt. Add the sugar and boil fast for 10 minutes. Then stir in the grated cocoanut and boil for another 10 minutes. Take off the heat, add the cream and beat well until it begins to set. Pour half quickly into a buttered soup plate. Add to the rest a drop of vanilla and a drop of cochineal. Pour on top of the other in the soup plate.

When cool cut into little shapes.   N.B. The first layer must be nearly set to take the weight of the second layer.   A recipe from the 1920s!

Cocoanut shortbread

    4 oz plain flour.   2½ oz butter.   1½ oz vanilla sugar
    1 dessertspoonful dessicated cocoanut.

Sieve the flour & the sugar and rub into the butter until like fine breadcrumbs. Add the cocoanut and mix in well. Well butter a tin and pour in the mixture. Spread evenly about ¼" thick. Firm with the base of a mug.

    Cook at No 3 for about 25 minutes.

    Score into shapes while still hot. These will break off easily when it is cold.   Other grated nuts may be used instead of cocoanut.

    Without nuts it is just plain shortbread. Vanilla sugar is made by keeping 2 pods in a jar and adding caster sugar from time to time. It greatly improves the flavour of most puddings if this sugar is used.

    I am sure you will enjoy adding crystallised fruits and the like to this mixture to enjoy after meals with your coffee.   Here are one or two quick puddings:

Creme Chantilly.

    1 oz double cream.   2 oz apple purée (Bramleys are best.) Sugar to taste.

    Whip the cream but be careful. It should not become butter. Stir in the apple & sugar the mixture. Pour into a glass and decorate with pieces of crystallised fruits or strawberries or raspberries or anything else suitable that takes your fancy!

Atholl Brose.   ¼ pt stiffly whipped cream.
　　　　　　　1 dessertspoon liquid honey.
　　　　　　　1 tablespoon coarse-ish oatmeal.
　　　　　　　1 tot scotch whisky.
Stir all the ingredients gently adding the whisky last.

Quick Orange Cheesecake.
　　½ lb cream cheese. 1 dessertspoonful caster sugar.
　　Juice of an orange. Rind, grated of ½ the orange.
　　2 tablespoons whipped cream.
Beat all together until creamy.   Make a base of crushed digestive biscuits in a small buttered tin. Add enough melted butter to hold the base together. (A teaspoon of golden syrup helps to stop the base crumbling.) Smooth the cheesecake on top of the base & refrigerate. This makes 3 generous portions & will keep in the fridge.

Syllabub. ¼ pt double cream. 1 lemon and the grated peel of ½ of it, 1 oz caster sugar. ½ glass sweet sherry or brandy.   Whip the cream with the peel. Add the juice, sugar & sherry. Whip very gently. Pour into 3 glasses (half the amounts makes one generous serving)

Commercial ice cream can be very good. Here are two sauces with which to ennoble it!

Raspberry sauce: 4 oz raspberries. 2 tablespoons sifted icing sugar.
Rub the fruit through the sieve, add the sugar and a very little Kirsch or other liqueur.

Chocolate sauce:
1 level dessertspoonful of cocoa.
½ "   "   corn flour.
1 level tablespoonful of vanilla sugar.
¼ pt water.   ¼ oz butter.

Smooth the corn flour with a little water. Gradually add and mix together very thoroughly all the ingredients. Bring to the boil stirring constantly and simmer for 2 minutes. Do not cease stirring.

If liked a tot of rum can be added to good effect!

Now for the final few pages. Here are two menus suitable for a little tête à tête dinner party using recipes from the book. They are put together in such a way that you can enjoy entertaining your guest but feel quietly confident that the dinner will be a success.

When Nubar Gulbenkian was asked his idea for a perfect dinner party he replied: "Myself and a good head waiter."

The one dish I find quite foolproof is Boeuf Wellington. 8-12 oz fillet steak bought in a piece will give 2 ample servings. It can be prepared hours in advance (p.52) and as long as the oven is preheated to gas Mark 7 will take exactly 35 minutes to cook. A minute timer is very useful. Once the dish is in the oven, with a glass in one hand, pleasant company and good conversation, 35 minutes flash by — The bell recalls one to reality!

Watercress soup (p.76) has a wonderful taste of oysters. It is very easy to make and will reheat without losing virtue. New potatoes are delicious with the rich meat dish & take 20 minutes. The broccoli only needs 8 minutes. A green salad (p.8) is even less demanding & will look attractive on the table.

Orange cheesecake (p.90) has a fresh tangy taste. That is ready in the fridge. Then, perhaps, some cheese to finish up the bottle of red wine?

If the electric kettle is full of boiling water it will shorten the time needed to look after the vegetables. Some french bread or rolls put into the oven when the broccoli goes into the pot will come out crisp and delicious in time for the soup.

Another foolproof dish is Petti di Pollo alla Valdestrama (p.60) (The two menus are shown overleaf). Writing a detailed menu is a great help. It makes it easier to compile an accurate shopping list and so not forget some silly little thing which would spoil the occasion.

Using smoked herring and Russian eggs (p.86) as a starter the time needed to complete the chicken dish is minimal. The preparing and initial cooking of the chicken can be done much earlier. Chicory will fry in a few minutes on low heat and does not need much watching (p.15). Pre-cooked rice will sit in a low oven. Just add a dessertspoonful of water, a knob of butter, and cover closely with foil.

Syllabub (p.90) is a party dish very easy to make. If you are not in splendid appetite some fresh fruit salad might be a wiser choice. A dry white wine would go well with the meal.

If you have a collection of the petits fours (p.87) they would come in to their own with a cup of coffee. Otherwise a box of chocolates would do just as well.

Hot Soup, Cold Meat or Fish, baked jacket potatoes and a good salad followed by a rum soufflé omelette (p.10) is another easy way to entertain. Simple things are usually best. You must enjoy your own party.

A good bottle of Burgundy

Watercress soup garnished
with cream & chopped watercress
crisp French Bread.

Boeuf Wellington with
New potatoes and Broccoli
or Green Salad.

Orange cheesecake

cheese

Coffee.

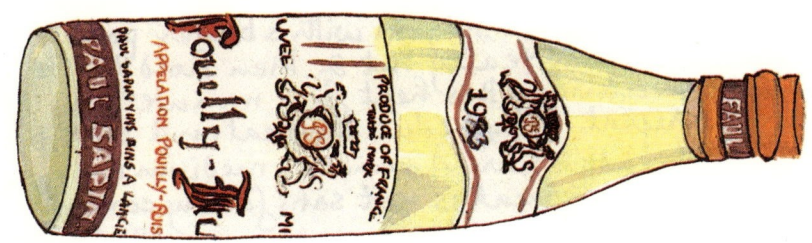

Smoked Herring, Russian Eggs, Brown bread and butter, garnished with lemon wedges.

Petti di Pollo alla Valdestramo
Rice, Green Salad, and French dressing.

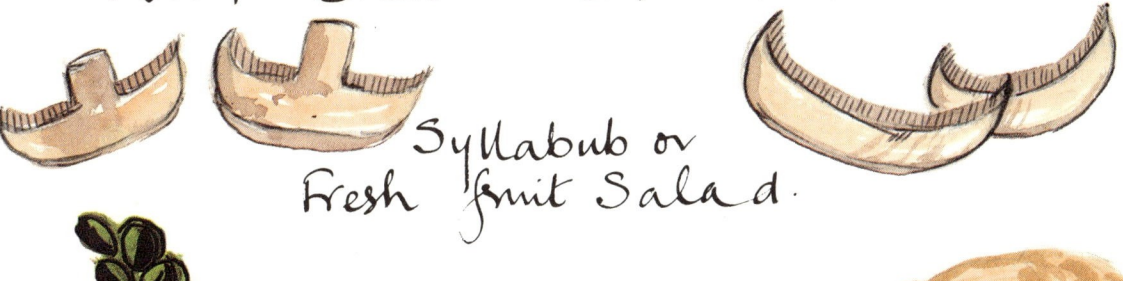

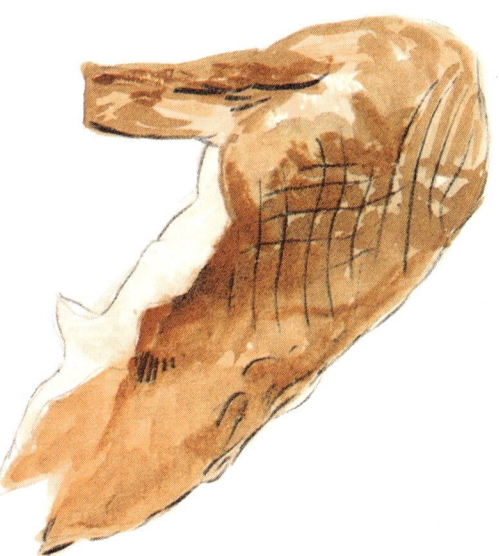

Syllabub or
Fresh fruit Salad.

Cheese

Coffee.

Dodges and Time savers.

When you boil an electric kettle just cover the element. If water is left over store in a thermos flask! Chopping parsley and other herbs is easiest in a cup using scissors. The herbs fall back from the sides as the scissors scythe through them. For mint sauce add a little sugar to the mint and it will chop more easily. Chopped sugary mint can be frozen in the ice tray and then stored in polythene in the ice compartment for "instant" mint sauce. As I peel vegetables I keep the unwanted bits: coarse leaves, stems, peels, coffee grounds, tea leaves, orange skins etc., in a jerry on the window sill. When this is full it goes out to the compost heap. Result rich compost, clean dustbin. Basil, that wonderful herb for Summer use with tomatoes, grows better in a flower pot on the south window sill than in the garden. A packet of seed is inexpensive. If you have an aluminium saucepan blackened through boiling water, put in apple peel or other acid waste and boil!

Beurre manié	p. 20 & 60	How to chop an onion	p. 82
Colander	p. 62	Keeping vegetables in the fridge	p. 24
Clover	p. 59/60	Oil pot and pastry brush	p. 55
Duxelle	p. 29 & 52	Seasoned flour	p. 54
French dressing	p. 8 & 68	Vanilla sugar	p. 89

EQUIVALENT MEASURES

I know it is now considered "with it" to think in grammes, metres and litres ~~ But women of my generation know the old measures by heart and will find it hard to change. I hope these conversion tables will prove useful. They are all <u>very</u> approximate and not meant to be taken as a firm fact.

The basis of measuring in cooking is founded on simple experience and on methods which have been proved to work.

For instance:

To make a pint of thin sauce (ie like single cream) use 1-2 oz butter, oil or fat, 1 oz plain flour and a pint of fluid.

To make a pint of thick sauce (ie like double cream) use 2-3 oz of fat, butter or oil, 2 oz plain flour and a pint of fluid.

To make a sauce of "blancmange" like consistency use 2 oz corn flour to a pint of fluid and enrich with butter.

My measuring CUP is a teacup ~ 6 fl. oz.

My measuring coffee CUP is about 3 fl. oz.

I am indebted to Peter E. Jones Esq., M.P.S., who supervised this tricky end paper. He warns us only to work in one scale at a time ~ never to mix them ~~